The Age of the
MAD DRAGONS

The Age of the
MAD DRAGONS

STEAM LOCOMOTIVES IN NORTH AMERICA

Douglas Waitley

BEAUFORT BOOKS, INC.
New York • Toronto

Excerpts reprinted with the permission of R.R. Donnelly
and Sons Company from the Lakeside Classic,
Growing up with Southern Illinois, by Daniel Brush.

Library of Congress Cataloging in Publication Data

Waitley, Douglas.
The age of the mad dragons.

Includes index.
SUMMARY: Covers the history of railroads from the 1830's
to the close of the 1930's.
1. Railroads—United States—History.   [1. Railroads—History] I. Title.
TF23.W34 1981   385'.0973   80-27242
ISBN 0-8253-0029-0

Published in the United States by Beaufort Books, Inc.,
New York. Published simultaneously in Canada by
Nelson, Foster and Scott Ltd.

Design: Ellen LoGiudice
Printed in the U.S.A.   First Edition
10   9   8   7   6   5   4   3   2   1

Contents

1. The First Mad Dragon   7

2. The Steam Pots   21

3. Upon the Wings of Lightning   37

4. Empire on the Prairies   59

5. The War Trains   81

6. The New World of Transcontinental Travel   103

7. Titan of the Rails   143

8. The Dragon Empire   163

9. The Wild Drama of Adventure   181

10. Song of the Rails   200

Afterword   220

Index   221

1

The First Mad Dragon

The old steam locomotives were like beasts from another dimension. The mad dragons, as Charles Dickens called them, were of metal made, but they were somehow alive. They hissed steam, spouted smoke, bellowed with an eerie reverberation that made the blood tingle. They sped boldly through the land, making the earth shake with their tread, leaving a tangy smell of smoke and a gritty film of cinders to serve notice that the universe was theirs.

And it was theirs—for a full century. The steam locomotives were kings—really kings, not just tolerated conveniences like the modern diesels. When a steam train rumbled past, it wasn't with a simple diesel hum and a monotonous grinding of unseen engine parts. The steamer chugged, manly and fiercely, and it meant business. Persons nearby could see the long steel piston rods jerking in and out of the steam cylinder, could see the massive connecting rods straining as they forced the drive wheels forward. They could actually witness the power of the machine, not passively imagine it as with modern locomotives.

When these steam kings entered a city or town, it was a real event. During most of their century-long reign, there were no other good means of transportation. It was take the train or ride a mule. Trains took loved ones away and brought them safely back. Trains ushered in flamboyant circuses and took them away. Trains brought in fresh vegetables from distant fields. Trains delivered exotic merchandise from worlds beyond the rim of the sea.

Steam locomotives were ninety years old before the radio made much of an impact on communications. During this long period of time, it was steam that brought big city newspapers to the surrounding country, steam that ended the age-long isolation. It was steam that carried politicians into the hinterlands, where few persons had ever seen those who governed them. It was steam that took the small towner to the cities, where he saw what life was all about.

Locomotives could make or break a community. Did a farmer wish to get his corn to market? Well, he must do so by train. Did a merchant wish to have a full line of the latest New York fashions? Well, he must import it by train. Did community leaders wish to attract new industries to their town? Well, they must assure them they had a rail outlet. Towns on rail lines became prosperous. Town off the lines stagnated, then decayed, and often died.

Yes, for a hundred years the mad dragons held America in subservience. To imagine the nation between 1830 and 1930 without steam locomotives would be the same as imagining an orchestra without its rhythm section. For the steamers were the heartbeat of the nation. The throb of the great steam-driven locomotive wheels on iron rails told the song of a nation on the move—building itself, flexing its economic muscles, reaching outward and onward toward its destiny.

To persons living during the era of the steam locomotives,

the big engines were more than dynamic expressions of national energy. They were personal experiences, often felt quite deeply. The railroad depot was easily the most important building in town. A visit to the depot was an experience that left an indelible impression on everyone, as it did on a young Chicagoan who has left us his impressions:

How well I remember walking with my parents through Chicago's Illinois Central depot! It was as large and mysterious as a cavern, over a hundred yards from end to end, with a massive ceiling that arched five stories overhead. The public address system echoed through the depot like the voice of God as it announced train arrivals and departures.

At the far end of the depot steps led down to the railroad tracks. Descending, we passed from the airy lobby to the track area. The change was startling. It was like entering a kind of mechanical Hades. Here machines, not man, reigned. The wooden canopies that hung over the walkways cut the rest of the world off. We were in a dark and forbidding place. We felt we were aliens—trespassers. Before us stood long rows of railroad cars—a solid underworld fortress. The air was bitter with smoke fumes, and cinders crunched like bones underfoot. My father was going on a trip and while my mother wished him goodbye, they ignored me for the moment. I walked hesitantly toward the locomotive, drawn to it as if by some hypnotic urge.

There were few humans at the head of the train, only a man oiling the wheels and the engineer, ghostly and unreal behind the cab window. I stood near the great engine. The drive wheels were twice as high as I was. They seemed so heavy that I had difficulty under-

9

standing how they could ever be moved. Then my eyes slid upward to the boiler. It towered over me almost menacingly. What if it should tip and crush me! I thought. Just then a thick cloud of steam sizzled from the locomotive's cylinder. It was water vapor, really, and not all that hot, but it startled me so that I leaped backward in fright.

The oil man tried to reassure me. But I felt that the locomotive wanted to show me his strength. I stood quite still, not wanting to make the big machine angry. The locomotive went "thunk, thunk, thunk." More steam hissed toward me. But I was used to it now. It seemed to say that the locomotive found me to its liking. Although I still feared the Thing, just as I would a lion who might spring, I felt that I had a kind of friend. The locomotive hissed and steamed and thunked and sent a pale stream of smoke into the air. It chugga-chugged, but didn't move. Yes, this monstrous concoction of steel, steam, and fire, I thought, was certainly alive. Although my mind told me it was not so, my heart, pounding with excitement and wonder, told me otherwise.

I walked back to my mother, who had grown alarmed over my disappearance. I saw my father in the coach. He looked startlingly small. With the window glass cutting off conversation, it was as if he was caught in the belly of the train. I had suddenly lost him. I felt lonely and alarmed.

Then the conductor yelled "All Aboard." A moment later the locomotive gave a violent "huff" which resounded down the walkway like a muffled cannon shot. The first "huff" was quickly followed by a second . . . and then a third. The coaches moved forward, slowly at first, then with increasing rapidity. Almost before I realized it my father was gone and a speeding succession of faces flashed before my eyes. There was a loud clack . . . clack . . . clack as the coach wheels clanged over the rail ends. Dust rose and the gush of passing cars made my eyes smart. On and on they came . . . coach after coach. The clacks got closer together and the wind became a gale. Now the walkway began to shake with the train's motion.

The coaches were a blur before me. Amid the turmoil I heard the locomotive whistle. It shrieked in triumph. The cars and passengers were his! Nothing of mere flesh and blood could stop his onward rush! He was a god unto himself!

To youths, such as myself, growing up during the age of the Mad Dragons it seemed as if the steam locomotives were among the Eternals—things that would be here for all time. So too were the great depots . . . the scream of the whistles . . . the lingering smell of coal smoke. It was impossible to understand that the steam locomotives, for all their power, were temporary creations. There would be a day, far sooner than anyone imagined, when the steamers would be herded off to railroad boneyards to become rejected, rusting hulks of a bygone era.

Yet, on the other side of history, so too was there a day when the steam locomotives were as yet unborn ideas churning through the minds of young men. There was a day when the concept of a steam engine driving coaches over iron rails was so new, so utterly beyond the comprehension of ordinary persons, as to be in the realm of the most breathtaking speculation. "Steam." The word sparked from the lips of souls with imagination. "S-s-steam." The word sizzled with energy. It was futuristic, the ultra in science. It conjured up shapes and sounds and concepts of motion and movement that a thousand prior generations had never known.

Back in the 1820's few persons had heard of locomotives. All that most persons knew was that steam engines were cumbersome things used to drive ships and heavy factory machinery. To set one of those fire-raging steam machines on wheels and speed it down a highway of rails—that was something only a few persons dreamed of. Among these was a businessman from Baltimore named Peter Cooper.

Peter Cooper had no all-consuming interest in the newfangled things that the canal men called sarcastically "steam pots." He made carriages mostly, although he had dabbled in the grocery line. the hattery field, and even stuck it out for a while in glue. Cooper's concern at the moment was with his large land investment on the outskirts of Baltimore. Should the city continue to grow, his real estate would soon be worth a fortune. But should the city stagnate, as was apparently about to happen, Cooper would suffer a distressing loss.

Baltimore's problem was that the city was unable to compete with Philadelphia and New York for the growing trade of the new states over the Appalachians. New York City, in particular, was prospering from the commerce brought to it over the Erie Canal, which opened in 1825 and connected the Hudson River with the Great Lakes. The citizens of Baltimore knew that they had no chance of constructing a canal through the humps of the Appalachians. So, instead, they had decided to run a set of rails over the mountains to the Ohio River three hundred miles away. Over this "rail road" horses would draw carts, wagons, and carriages.

The Baltimore and Ohio Railroad had been organized in 1827 to build the first general freight and passenger line in the United States. Baltimore citizens invested heavily in the B&O, and by July 4 of the following year sufficient funds were available to begin work on the ambitious project. Ground-breaking ceremonies took place amid boisterous fanfare, a salute by Old Ironsides, and a brief speech by tottering Charles Carroll, last surviving signer of the Declaration of Independence.

Despite the hoopla, the B&O quickly ran into trouble. The greatest difficulty was with the horses, who were placed inside the vehicle and moved it forward by plodding over an endless tread connected with the wheels. Not only did the passengers ride with manure and horseflies, but the pace was very slow—for locomotion of only a single horsepower was little better than putting a sail on the car and letting the wind push it (which was also tried).

The horsecars even had problems holding their own against cows on the tracks. In at least once instance of a car-cow collision, it was the coach rather than bossie which skidded off the track and bounced down an embankment. To be thrown by a family cow was a humiliating way to terminate a ride, and the B&O's passenger service did not prove to be especially popular.

It was now that Peter Cooper entered the picture. The land speculator, worried that the B&O would fail, urged the rail-road directors to consider using one of those radical new British steam engines to pull their coaches. Cooper was convinced it would do the job, for a steam locomotive had hauled granite blocks for Boston's Bunker Hill Monument three miles from the quarry site back in 1826.

The railroad directors smiled condescendingly. Three miles? What was that compared to the 300 miles they planned? Why, a steam-pot locomotive would either fall apart or blow itself up long before reaching its destination. Besides, they added, experience in Britain had indicated that locomotives could not maneuver around curves with less than a 300-foot radius. The B&O had many curves of a mere 150-foot radius.

Nevertheless, Peter Cooper persisted. Why not import a locomotive from England (there were none being built at the moment in the United States) and give it a trial? When the directors again rejected the idea as preposterous as well as expensive, Cooper decided to build his own locomotive to show them it could function on their tracks.

Cooper had in his factory a piston cylinder only three inches in diameter he used as a water pump. Hoping it was strong enough to pull a passenger car, he loaded it onto a horse cart and carried it to the B&O shop. Once there he hunted up some iron plates amid the dusty debris in the shop and hammered them into a boiler a couple of feet wide and some three feet high.

After the exterior of the boiler was completed, Cooper inserted a cross plate about two thirds down the interior. The upper portion would hold water, and the lower portion would be a firebox in which he would burn the wood which would cause the water to boil. Since the smoke would need to escape, Cooper drilled a series of holes in the plate that separated the two portions of the boiler and into these holes he placed cooper tubes, extending upward through the water to the smokestack. These flues were made of copper so that they could easily transmit the heat from the smoke and hot air to the surrounding water. But, since the copper flues were small and the smoke would not pass readily up them, Cooper installed a fan near the top of the smokestack to suck the smoke up the flues. This fan was driven by a belt attached to the wheel axles.

Cooper knew that after the fire began and the water started to boil, it would build up pressure in the upper part of the boiler. The pressure must not become too great or it would cause the boiler to explode. Therefore Cooper put a safety valve near the top of the boiler. When the pressure approached a dangerous level, the safety valve would pop open to release the steam.

When it came time to find iron pipes to convey the steam from the top of the boiler to the cylinder down by the wheels, Cooper ran into a problem. There were no factories where he could get engine parts. "I couldn't find any iron pipes," Cooper recalled. "The fact was, there were none for sale in this country. So I took two muskets, broke off the wooden parts, and used the barrels for tubing." Scrounging for more parts, Cooper inserted a throttle valve within the upper musket barrel. By means of a lever attached to the valve, he could control how much steam flowed from the boiler to the cylinder. The wider he opened the valve, the more steam flowed, and the more steam flowed, the faster the piston within the cylinder would propel the wheels.

On top of the cylinder was a boxlike affair called the steam chest, which the steam entered just before it entered the cylinder. Within the chest was a valve that covered one of two openings into the cylinder. The steam hissed through the opening that was not covered. Then, impelled by the pressure in the boiler, the steam pushed violently against the piston within the cylinder. As the piston was hurled across the cylinder, the air already in the chamber was pushed up with a chugging sound through the other opening in the cylinder. The slide valve did not permit the air to enter the steam chest. Instead, a hollow in the bottom part of the valve routed the air through an exhaust tube and out the side of the chest.

When the stroke was completed, the slide valve would move to cover the first opening and expose the second. Steam would enter the cylinder from the other direction, causing the piston to hurl backward. By alternate moves of the slide valve the piston would thus rush back and forth within the cylinder.

Attached to the piston was a rod. At its other end this piston rod was fastened to a small plate, called the crosshead, which slid along a pair of bars. A connecting rod was also attached to the moving crosshead. This connecting rod ran to the edge of one of the wheels, imparting to it the motion of the piston. It caused the wheels to turn and the locomotive to move.

Friends could not help but chuckle as Cooper's odd contraption began to take shape. "As I recall its appearance," one of his friends commented, "my only wonder is that so apparently insignificant a contrivance should ever have been regarded as competent to the smallest results." Cooper, too, was amused with the engine and called it the *Tom Thumb*, after the tiny hero of English folk tales.

When the *Tom Thumb* was at last capable of some movement, Cooper invited the B&O president and some other officials to watch him run the little machine across the roundhouse. Cooper got a good blaze going and hesitantly drew the throttle lever down. The *Tom Thumb* shuddered as the piston chugged forward. The piston rod squeaked along the crosshead bar, and the connecting rod groaned and moved. Then, with a creak of wood and jangle of metal, the wheels made a half turn. The visitors watched as the little locomotive staggered across the wooden floor. It was a nice little trick of science, but hardly inspiring to a company requiring a means of propulsion that would travel not a few yards but a full 300 miles. Even a few days later, after Cooper managed to hoist his locomotive onto the B&O tracks and take the president a few hundred more yards along the right-of-way, most B&O officials were not impressed. For it was obvious that the steam toy would never be able to pull a heavy coach filled with passengers.

But Cooper himself was confident. He now made plans for a formal run all the way to Ellicott's Mills, thirteen miles from Baltimore. And this time he would pull a coach. But shortly before the epic journey, someone found the *Tom Thumb* parked outside the roundhouse and knocked off the smokestack and stole all the copper tubes from inside the boiler. It took Cooper a week to round up more tubes and replace them in the boiler.

He stored the locomotive inside now. But a curiosity seeker managed to break into the shop and roll one of the wheels around until he broke it. Cooper had another wheel cast, but it came out lopsided. So, too, did a second wheel. "Thought I," Cooper wrote, "the fates are against me! I was thoroughly disgusted and discouraged." Nevertheless he doggedly continued working, and the day finally came when he was ready for the official launching.

As the B&O officials gathered on the morning of September 18, 1830, they could not help but be disappointed at the sight. The *Tom Thumb* was a silly looking affair—just a homemade boiler, smaller than that which heated bathtub water, mounted on a slapdash wheeled platform. There was no cabin to protect Cooper should it rain. There was no whistle to warn animals or humans out of the way. There weren't even any brakes—only the drag of the engine to slow the train. The silliest thing of all was the cylinder, which was supposed to drive the locomotive and the heavy Conestoga wagon, which had been converted to a railroad coach by the simple addition of flanged wheels. Why, the cylinder was no wider than a man's fist! Amusement played over many faces. Why not humor good old Peter? The officials would just sit in his train until he admitted that his lilliput locomotive could not haul them all the way to Ellicott's Mills. It was a little crowded, however, with thirty-six of them jammed in the wagon and an overflow of six, standing elbow to elbow on the cramped platform of the locomotive itself.

Cooper worked around the men on the platform. He managed to get a load of logs in the boiler and soon had a nice fire going. After a while the water above the fire heated, and eventually steam was singing from the safety valve at the top of the boiler.

The riders grew silent as Cooper pulled the throttle. They heard the steam sizzle through the old musket barrels into the steam chest. Quickly the steam flooded into the cylinder. There was a chug as the piston rod was forced forward. The piston rod slid along the crosshead bars. As the crosshead moved, the connecting rod was pushed forward, and the wheel turned. Then the slide valve within the steam chest closed one opening into the cylinder and uncovered the other. The piston moved in the opposite direction and the wheel groaned forward again. The chug-chug grew more rapid. The wheels turned more quickly. The *Tom Thumb* actually caused the heavy Conestoga to roll along the tracks.

In disbelief, the passengers leaned over the wagon to watch the wheels turn. Then they grinned at one another. Their grins broadened· as the *Tom Thumb* slowly gained speed. It rounded one of the 150-foot radius curves and ascended an upgrade with ease. The officials and their friends cheered. A steam locomotive could run on the B&O tracks. The railroad was saved. Saved, too, Cooper must have mused, were his land investments.

The rest of the thirteen-mile trip to Ellicott's Mills was pure joy. The *Tom Thumb* chug-a-chugged over the glittering tracks with a speed that at times reached a fantastic eighteen miles per hour. Only those passengers who had ridden race horses had ever gone that fast. Yet to compare the ride with that of a galloping horse was impossible. Rail travel was so smooth that one could actually write a letter while moving, as several men proved to the others by doing so.

The directors rose from their seats and milled around the wagon. Even though they were crowded, it was still infinitely more comfortable than riding in a stagecoach where passengers could not stretch their legs—to say nothing of actually walking about. And a stagecoach was lucky to average much more than three miles an hour.

But the stage operators were not ready to have their lines made obsolete. On the way back from Ellicott's Mills, Cooper was met by a representative of the Stockton & Stokes Stage Line. The stage driver challenged Cooper to a race. A Stockton stagecoach had been set on one of the pair of rails leading to Baltimore, and the huge gray horse hitched to the coach was impatient to be off. Cooper accepted, and the race was on.

While the *Tom Thumb* was slowly gathering speed, the horse leaped to a handsome lead. Cooper stuffed more wood into the firebox, for he did not intend to have his triumphant moment tarnished by a nag and a boastful horseman. Showers of sparks were thrown into the air by the blower fan on the smokestack. Gradually the steam pressure rose. Finally a shrill whistle from the safety valve announced that the pressure was fully up. Now *Tom Thumb*'s speed increased. The locomotive began gaining on the stagecoach, which was still about a quarter mile ahead:

The steam blew off in vapory clouds, the pace increased [recalled John Latrobe, one of Cooper's riders] the passengers shouted, and the engine gained on the horse. Soon the race was neck and neck, nose and nose—then the engine passed the horse, and a great hurrah hailed the victory. But it was not repeated, for just at this time, when the gray's master was about giving up, the band that drove the pulley that drove the blower slipped off its drum. The safety valve ceased to scream, and the engine for want of breath began to wheeze and pant.

Cooper frantically attempted to replace the pulley on the blower drum. Both the blower and the pulley were frightfully hot. Cooper winced as burns welted on his fingers. He tried several times, but failed. Meanwhile the fire fumes refused to go up the narrow flues. The water began cooling, and the steam pressure continued dropping. *Tom Thumb*'s speed diminished.

The stagecoach driver overtook the locomotive with a proper raspberry salute to the passengers. As he stretched his lead, Cooper continued working furiously on the blower pulley. At last he had it attached. But it was too late. By the time Cooper got his steam pressure up the horse had charged across the finish line.

That the nation's first American-made locomotive had been beaten by a horse did not overly dampen the enthusiasm of the moment. The fact remained that no horse could have covered the entire twenty-six mile round trip at an average speed of nearly fourteen miles an hour—as the *Tom Thumb* had. Furthermore, Cooper had demonstrated that steam trains could operate on the narrow B&O curves. Although the *Tom Thumb* itself was too small for sustained use, it had clearly set the stage for larger engines.

On that autumn day in 1830 the Age of the Mad Dragons had begun.

2

The Steam Pots

C harles Dickens stared, fascinated, through a window in the passenger car. It was 1842, and to ride an express train was one of the most thrilling experiences a person of sturdy constitution could enjoy.

On the train whirls headlong [Dickens wrote in his *American Notes*], it dives through the woods, emerges in the light, clatters over frail arches, rumbles upon the heavy ground, shoots beneath a wooden bridge which intercepts the light for a second like a wink, suddenly awakens all the slumbering echoes in the main street of a large town, and dashes on hap-hazard, pell-mell, neck or nothing, down the middle of the road.

Dickens could not take his eyes from the landscape rushing past. Now the train sped through the untamed forest down a roadcut so narrow that leaves and twigs spattered against the window. Beyond he caught glimpses of huge tree trunks, a canopy of verdant oak and maple leaves, and beneath them a jumble of underbrush and rotting logs. Then, with a suddenness which made him catch his breath, the forest was gone and the train broke into farmlands:

Now you emerge for a few brief minutes on an open country, glittering with some bright lake or pool, broad as many an English river, but so small here that it scarcely has a name; now you catch hasty glimpses of a distant town, with its clean white houses and their cool piazzas, its prim New England church and schoolhouse; when whir-r-r-r! almost before you have seen them, comes the same dark forest screen. . . .

When Dickens arrived in the United States in 1842, he found himself in the midst of what could only be called a railroad mania. The B&O engines had hardly started running between Baltimore and Frederick, Maryland, before every town of consequence, and many of no consequence, began agitating for railroads of their own. Every little cluster of cabins thought that if it just obtained a railroad to bring settlers in and carry farm produce out it could become another Baltimore. By 1840 there were several hundred rail lines either being operated or under construction. Most of them were short little things, running from a settlement to a river or seaport. Some were more ambitious though, like the B&O which was slowly, ever so slowly, worming its way over the Maryland mountains toward Wheeling on the Ohio River, which it was not to reach for an agonizing quarter century. The Pennsylvania Railroad was another greatly heralded enterprise—instigated by the citizens of Philadelphia, who were concerned that Baltimore would snatch their trade with the interior.

Railroad lines began to unravel like strands of spaghetti during the 1830's and 40's. Great were the celebrations when the first steam pot made its appearance in town. Sayward Luckett, aging heroine of Conrad Richter's Pulitzer Prize winning novel, *The Town*, was among the old-timers at such a celebration. She viewed the huge iron engine, freighted in on a riverboat, with fear as well as awe: "Black and besotted, with a vicious iron point in front to cut you to pieces and a fierce stack belching smoke and fire, it looked like it came from where canal folks claimed, the pits of hell"—such was Sayward's opinion of the thing.

Yet most citizens of Sayward's little Ohio town were tremendously elated that they now had a railroad, even though the rails ran only for a few miles. The highlight of the rail-opening celebration involved starting the locomotive. Young boys happily scurried back and forth with buckets of water to fill the boiler. Meanwhile their fathers carted in stacks of wood. Then everyone gathered around the impressive machine while the engineer worked up a fire.

The assembly grew silent as the fire grew. Soon a faint trail of gray smoke began trailing up from the smokestack. Then they heard it—quietly at first, hardly more than a faint hiss—steam issuing from the safety valve. And although the locomotive remained stationary, everyone knew that the steam had breathed life into it.

"Clear the track," the engineer yelled as he pulled the throttle. "At last slowly with hoots and screechings and a great hissing and grunting, the engine began to move," Richter wrote. "Dogs dropped their tails between their legs and ran off howling, while men in front of the engine cleared ditches and fences at a single bound." There was an instinctive fear of the monstrous machine—its strangeness, its power, its unpredict-ability. It was an alien creature, untamed. The railroad ties bent as the massive machine moved over them, gradually picking up speed. The ground trembled slightly. The air became dark as smoke momentarily hid the sun. Sparks and charred wood rained on the spectators, causing both men and women to shout angrily as holes smoldered in their clothing.

As the locomotive moved on down the street, the crowd's self-confidence returned. There were cheers and nods of ap-proval. The engineer stopped the locomotive after a few blocks. Then an open car was attached with the town's most important citizens in it. The train returned to the site of the festivities, where the dignitaries gave fine speeches about the glories that the railroad would bring the town. When they were through, food and hard cider were broken out. The celebration lasted far into the night, and the hangovers into the next day. It was an experience no one would ever forget—the day the locomotive came to town.

Of course just because a hamlet had a steam pot didn't necessarily mean the fool contraption was good for anything. Many railroads ran from no place to no place. As a result, nobody rode on them, and nobody kept them up.

A vivid account of one such railroad has been left us by Daniel Brush, taking a train in frontier Illinois around 1839. This railroad was part of the state's overly ambitious scheme for more than a thousand miles of rails across Illinois. The Panic of 1837 ended that fantasy, leaving Illinois with a stag-gering debt and only a few miles of creaky track.

Mr. Brush had flatboated down the Illinois River after an excursion to the bustling little settlement on Lake Michigan known as Chicago. When he got to Beardstown, he decided to take the train that meandered across the prairie to Springfield. He should have been forewarned, since the train consisted of only a dilapidated locomotive and a single passenger car that had no roof or even sides. The railroad track was of wooden rails with a thin strip of iron crudely nailed to the top. Brush nonetheless boarded the flatcar, and soon the locomotive staggered out of the ramshackle station:

The dimunitive engine made a start with myself and perhaps another man or two as passengers. Feebly it cleared the outskirts of the town and up the river's second bank, and finally with weakened energy reached the broad prairie that spread out expansively towards the point of destination.

Troubles soon presented themselves to obstruct progress. The ties were loosely put down and wobbled out of line. The flat half-inch bar-iron laid to guide the wheels over the wooden rails became loosened at the ends and turned up, thrusting "snake heads" through the bottom of the car and jolting the unwary passenger by a murderous dig into his anatomy if he happened to be in its way.

Then steam became low, and the engine had to be cut loose and paraded up and down the wobbling track to recuperate strength and power sufficient to proceed.

It was very slow going. When twilight came, the train's puffing stopped, since it had no lights for night traveling. Dan Brush had his choice of sleeping on the lumpy wooden flatcar floor or hoofing it on his own. He left the incompetent locomotive in the midst of the prairie and walked the remaining eight miles to his home. He could be forgiven if he doubted the future of steam travel.

Such, however, was not the case with the majority of Americans. Everywhere across the nation steam-pot locomotives became the rage. Pictures of them were used as decorations on china plates and on the finest drinking glasses. Housewives put colorful trains on the samplers that they hung in the family living room. Menfolk told railroad stories over farm fences or around the general store. Grandmaw and grandpaw wrote letters to their sons and daughters urging them to come and visit, and bring the kids, now that the rail line had converted a two-day horse saga into a four-hour pleasure jaunt.

Newspapers were filled with accounts of the successes of established railroads and of the completions of new ones. President John Quincy Adams himself broke the sod for the Chesapeake & Ohio, designed to do for Richmond, Virginia, what the B&O was about to do for Baltimore and the Pennsy for Philadelphia. Across the Appalachians, railroad activity was just as intense. In the five-year period just prior to 1840, Indiana alone chartered twenty-five lines.

No one was immune from the railroad fever of the 1830's and 1840's. Even Henry Thoreau, Concord's nature-loving philosopher. was entranced by the steam pots. Living in a cabin that he had built beside Walden pond in Massachusetts, Thoreau watched the daily freight trains skirt the pond as they carried goods between Boston and Lake Champlain. The trains were to Thoreau as entrancing as the thrushes that sang from the boughs or the perch that swarmed around his boat when he plaved his flute in the moonlight.

The railroad became part of Thoreau's Walden adventure. "The whistle of the locomotive penetrates my woods summer and winter," Thoreau wrote, "sounding like the scream of a hawk." Thoreau often saw the trains up close, for on his regular trips to Concord he preferred walking on the level railroad embankment to trodding the rutted farmer's road. Many times he jumped off the tracks for the locomotive to pass by at twenty miles an hour. His eyes smarted from the smoke, his skin prickled from the sparks, his ears rang from the sound of the bell, his body trembled slightly from the earth vibrating beneath him. But he didn't find the sensations disagreeable. Instead, he confessed, "I am refreshed and expanded when the freight train rattles past me."

For all his enthrallment with nature, Thoreau was tremendously impressed with man's genius at building a machine which, to some extent, conquered the natural elements. The iron horse was a mighty beast. Fire flamed in his breast. The hills resounded with his snorting. He ate vast quantities of wood and drank uncountable gallons of water. He moved like an avalanche, shrinking time and distance, shrinking the earth itself. With the advent of the locomotives, Thoreau mused, "the earth has got a race now worthy to inhabit it."

To Thoreau even locomotive smoke had a distinctive beauty. "I watch the passage of the morning cars with the same feeling that I do the rising of the sun, which is hardly more regular. The locomotive's train of clouds stretching far behind and rising higher and higher, going to heaven while the cars are going to Boston, conceals the sun for a minute and casts my distant field into the shade."

Thoreau saw more to the railroads than the individual trains that wooshed through his little domain like comets toward celestial infinity. When walking the rails, he could smell the goods on the freight cars. And when he did, he was reminded of coral reefs and African deserts and churning fishing banks in the North Atlantic. The world was riding on the back of the iron horse, entering the hitherto isolated farms and hamlets of New England. Breathing new life into them. Now his fellow New Englanders could experience luxuries that originated half a world away. And Yankees, for their part, could freight their grain to Boston, where merchants would continue the exchange that spanned thousands of leagues over blue water and purple headlands. The locomotives were bringing the nations of the world closer together.

Railroads were also changing men's ways of thought—and for the better, Thoreau believed. "The arrivals of the cars are now epochs in the village day," he noted. Timetables brought a new punctuality to the lackadaisical countryside. When the train departed, one had better have loaded his goods and himself on it or he would be left in the station. Thoreau even surmised that men talked and thought faster than they did before the railroad displaced the stagecoach. Persons were traveling much more, too, and thereby broadening their knowledge. "I have been astonished at the miracles the railroad has wrought," he commented. To do things "railroad fashion" was becoming a byword for modern efficiency. To be "on the right track" was everyone's goal. All in all, Thoreau believed, the train had brought a decided improvement in American life. "We live the steadier for it," was his final verdict.

Yet despite the unquestioned benefits ushered in by the steam pots, there were dangers and discomforts. As early as 1840 S. A. Howland published a gory book on railroad disasters and other "thrilling incidents," as he called them. Even though the railroad age was only a few years old Howland was able to chronicle fifteen rail accidents between 1836 and the first months of 1840.

There was, for example, the accident at Bridgeport, Connecticut. Some four hundred persons celebrated the opening of the railroad by taking a ride on one of the trains. Trains at this time had no centrally operated brakes, but were stopped by hand twisting brake wheels on each car. Somehow the brakemen forgot which direction to set the brakes. The train, on its very first day, consequently plowed off the end of the track and into an immense pile of rubbish. There were many broken arms, legs, wrists, etc., which, as the account concludes, "destroyed the hilarity of the occasion."

There was another crash near Burlington, New Jersey. "In a dense fog," Howland tells us, "the lumber cars from Camden met the passenger cars about three miles above Burlington. The locomotives came in contact, heads on, producing, as may well be imagined, a tremendous crash!" The engineers and firemen of both locomotives jumped just before the crash, but for the passengers "a bruise here and there betokened that a shock of no slight nature had occurred."

Often the subjects of accidents did not get off with just bruises. There was the train heading for Springfield, Massachusetts, which "came in contact with Mr. Hale Young." Mr. Young's ears were muffled against the cold, and a high snowbank hid the approaching engine. The "contact," as Howland so quaintly puts it, between Mr. Young and the locomotive was decisive and fatal for Mr. Young.

Railroad crossings were a constant source of danger. There was the case of Aaron Pratt, age seventy-five. Although the engineer and his passengers yelled for him to get off the tracks, he ignored them. The engineer made no attempt to slow down. People were constantly sauntering down the railroad right-of-way, since it was easier walking than the muddy roads. It wasn't until the engineer was almost on Mr. Pratt that he realized the old man was deaf. . . .

Then, too, rail builders often put pillars too close to the passing cars, as happened in the case of James F. Curtis, Esquire, who put his head out the window just as the train was passing beneath a bridge in Boston. . . .

And there were always hotshot engineers, such as the daredevil who left a rail turn-out and tried to speed down a single track segment before the express from Dedham met him from the opposite direction. The express was early and. . . .

Or the happy-go-lucky engineer of a fifteen-car lumber train racing down a long embankment, glorying in his break-neck speed—until he careened around a bend and saw a locomotive with two hundred passengers chugging up the single track toward him. . . .

Human errors accounted for a majority of the wrecks. Sometimes the blunders were so stupid as to make us blink. There was the case of the trainman taking his steam pot into New York City. It was the Fourth of July, and Engineer Spencer had had more than his fill of white lightning. Not as alert as usual, Spencer ran over a half-turned switch, thereby derailing his slow-moving locomotive. A number of persons, using wood posts, attempted to lift the steam pot back onto the tracks. Spencer, distracted from his supervision of this feat by the whistling safety valve, fastened it shut. It was quiet for a while—until the boiler blew up. Fifteen or twenty persons were either killed or severely scalded. Engineer Spencer did not care, for his concerns were no longer of this world. "His legs went into Union Park and his arms on to a pile of lumber"—so Mr. Howland tells us, taking his usual delight in tales of gore.

Accidents also came from poor bridge construction—not surprisingly. since locomotives were far heavier machines than the ordinary bridge could support. Although railroad bridges were built more solidly than wagon bridges, the architects used wood, for it was the cheapest and handiest material. Wood had the unfortunate tendency to rot, and the upshot was a series of incidents like that which took place in New York on May 3, 1840, when a bridge collapsed with five railroad cars passing over it. "The crash was tremendous," Howland continues, and forty persons along with all their most precious belongings went bobbing down a rain-swollen stream.

Early railroad planners did not realize the tremendous momentum that trains could gather. In 1839 officials of the

Camden and Amboy line thought that a train could be stopped at the rail's end by a couple of cowhides stretched between posts a foot and a half thick. They were quickly shown their error when an eight-car train snapped the posts "like pipe-stems," and the runaway train jolted down an embankment toward some steamboats docked below. Fortunately the embankment was used as a dump, and piles of garbage became caught beneath the wheels, forcing the cars to a skidding, stinking halt.

Immediately after the accident the passengers gathered in an angry meeting. Even in a day when railroad disasters were becoming increasingly common, the group declared that to attempt to stop a train by means of a few animal hides was "trifling with the lives of passengers unparalleled in its atrocity in the history of public conveyance." Thus relieving themselves of their anger, the passengers went home. Nothing more was heard of the incident.

It was not bad enough that locomotives were blowing up, brakes were being mishandled, bridges were collapsing, and trains were crashing into one another. The very rails over which the trains ran were often a hazard. The spikes which held them to the wooden ties sometimes worked loose, because of the constant jarring of passing cars. When this happened, the weight of the cars in the center of the rail would force the loose end up. It would then catch on the wheel of the following car and be forced through the floorboards. It was an unnerving experience to see the rail come crashing into the passenger section and on through the ceiling. These "snake-heads," as they were called, could gut an entire car in a matter of seconds.

The men who drove the primitive steam pots of the 1830's and 40's were reckless individuals who thrived not only on the challenge of engineering, but who gloried in the admiration that society felt for them. To say that one was an engineer was enough to cause lesser men to bite their lips as they compared their humdrum lives to the exciting escapades of those who raced across the country on steam pots.

Charlie Frisbie was a handsome youngster of fifteen when he found that the clack of steam-pot wheels was in his blood. His first job was in 1837 on the rail line at Quincy, Massachusetts. He soon quit the Quincy line and bounced around the Mohawk valley railroads, signing on as a fireman helper whenever there was a place open. It was only part-time work and very low on the scale of railroad prestige. But it was about the only thing a teenager could get. It didn't matter to Charlie—not so long as he was around the locomotives and the repair shops and the roundhouses that he loved.

One day Charlie pulled up stakes and went to New York City. From a floor sweeper at the depot he learned that a locomotive on the New Jersey Central needed a full-time assistant fireman. He dashed to the railroad office, convinced the superintendent of his fitness, and within three minutes had his first regular job. As assistant, he passed wood to the fireman, who threw it to the best spot in the firebox. Charlie got $20 per month for his work; the fireman got $25; and the engineer $50—more than Charlie and the fireman combined. That was a fair indication of the esteem in which an engineer was held.

Charlie's engine was small even by standards of the time, with only a single cylinder just fourteen inches wide (this was, nevertheless, four times larger than the midget cylinder on Peter Cooper's *Tom Thumb*). The locomotive was so weak that it could barely pull three cars on its short treks between Jersey City and New Brunswick. These cars were little more than stagecoaches fitted with flanged wheels. Their springs were simply leather harnesses six inches wide which supported the coach body between the axles. When the coach hit a bump, the harness lurched upward, and the passengers bounced off the ceiling.

Charlie soon yearned for the big time. So he quit the Jersey Central and, after a while, ended up as an engineer on the Michigan Central, which ran for about 100 miles between Detroit and Kalamazoo. Locomotives were in a constant state of change during the years that Charlie moved from job to job. We do not know what kind of locomotive Charlie drove for the MC, but we do know that he graduated from the old steam pots to a more modern type of locomotive with a cabin on the rear end to give him shelter from the wind and rain.

Train designers during the 1840's were doing more than just providing engineers and firemen with the luxury of a cabin. Indeed, their main interest was not the train crew but how to give the locomotive more speed and more power. The obvious way was to make the boiler larger. But it was clearly impractical to raise the boiler up too high, for this would cause the locomotive to wobble like a clown when it was moving. So, instead, the designers turned the boiler on its side, with the flues running parallel with the tracks. The smoke box was then placed in front, rather than on top, of the boiler flues. This way the boiler could be made as long as needed.

It was a fortunate solution to the problem in more ways than one, for it was found that after the steam left the cylinder it could now be routed up the smokestack instead of leaving by means of a useless exhaust tube. This escaping steam created a partial vacuum in the smoke box that sucked up the smoke from the firebox. Thus the new locomotives did not have to depend on the types of blower fans that had caused Peter Cooper to lose his race with the horse.

As the locomotives grew longer, designers had to add more wheels, both to support the extended boiler and to give the increasingly heavier engine more traction on the rails. Smallish "truck" wheels were placed under the smoke box and cylinders in the front. Toward the rear two larger wheels were placed. One of these wheels was connected to the piston by the main rod. The other wheel was joined to the first by a side rod. Thus the new locomotives had two drive wheels on each side rather than just one. To convey this information, a new rail lingo sprang up. These locomotives were designated as 4-4's— referring to the four front truck wheels and the four drive wheels. When a couple of truck wheels were added to later locomotives to support the cab, those locomotives were called 4-4-2's.

Other refinements occurred during these years. The smokestacks became huge inverted cones. This snappy touch was not merely for appearance. Locomotive designers had become concerned about the dangerous fountain of sparks that the wood-burning locomotives left in their wake. Therefore they placed spark-catching devices within the smokestacks, and the new shape accommodated the smokestack to this important innovation.

The train that Charlie drove was probably a small 2-4 (two front truck wheels and four drive wheels). Engines were very individual machines, no two alike. Charlie believed he had a bad-luck engine. All locomotives of that era had names, and Charlie's was called the *May Flower*, after a magnificent Lake Erie steamer that had sunk three times, the last forever. The first winter that Charlie was running the *May Flower* she ran off the tracks at Dexter, Michigan, and came chugging right up main street over the frozen earth. As the townsfolk watched in startled disbelief, then in fear for their lives, the *May Flower* began tipping this way and that as she sent rocks and frozen dirt shooting in all directions from her iron wheels. Charlie clutched whatever he could as the *May Flower* swayed dizzily. At last, after hurtling forward for fifty feet, she toppled onto her side. Steam spouted from all over, and the citizens ran for cover, fearing an explosion. "And where was I?" Charlie wrote with his usual twinkle. "Under her, of course, caught by my left foot with steam blowing on it." The steam may have saved his life though—or at least his leg. "My foot was on the ice, and the steam thawed it loose," Charlie recalled. He scrambled away from the hissing monster.

Charlie's experiences with the malicious locomotive were not over:

Another time I started with the same *May Flower* engine, and when three miles out from Marshall, Michigan, I ran into an ox, which threw the engine and train, every wheel, from the track. The engine rolled over twice and a half and lay on her back, fifty feet from the track, headed the opposite way. I looked around and found myself, and on taking an inventory, I found one arm disabled, my face and hands scalded, and my shoulder and collar bone broken. The fireman, poor fellow, fared much worse, and died in a few days. Now, tell me what's in a name? You may laugh, but I left the fated *May Flower* then and forever.

The Michigan Central paid Charlie's doctor bills and a full year's wages while he recovered. But it was money well spent, for it was not long before the company needed loyal men like Charlie. The trouble was with the farmers whose cattle were bumped by MC trains. Whether the animal was just grazed or was actually killed, the owners sent the MC a bill for its replacement. The MC, unable to sort the legitimate claims from those which bent the truth, adopted a simple formula for settlement. The company refused to pay any claims at all. This, as may be expected, disturbed the farmers greatly.

Toward the end of the 1840's the farmers took the offensive. A stretch of track about twenty miles long became a sort of no-man's-land. Only the bravest of the engineers dared take their trains through. Charles was one of these. More than once, as he clipped along the dangerous area around Niles, he rounded a bend and had to grind to a hasty stop to avoid being burned to death by a timber fire across the tracks.

At night it was worse. The farmers, who had been cautious about being identified in the daylight, could now stand in the shadows and hurl rocks at the train. Once in a while there would be the ominous snap of a rifle. Then Charlie would jump down from his exposed position in the cab to lie against the iron driving wheel guard. Meanwhile the train rushed down the perilous tracks with no one at the throttle.

The Michigan Central could do nothing until it found out who the ringleaders were. It took two years, but informants infiltrated the gang. Forty men were arrested, and ten were sent to prison. With the excitement over, Charlie drifted west to run engines on the prairies. But that's another story. . . .

3

Upon the Wings
of Lightning

Glasses clinked in Jones's Tavern as the men of Jamestown, New York, gathered for an important confab.
The excited undertone dwindled as the first speaker
rose to address the friends and neighbors who had come to
this hamlet on New York's far western frontier.

The subject was railroads, and the date was September,
1831. Jamestown, like other communities in the southern tier
of New York counties, had been bypassed by the successful
Erie Canal, opened six years earlier in central New York.
Feeling slighted, citizens of the area turned to the new railroads for help. Even though the nation's premier line, the
Baltimore and Ohio, had a mere fourteen miles of track in
operation, they could foresee the tremendous changes a rail
connection would bring to their region. They could send their
grain and other produce to the New York City market infinitely quicker and more cheaply than by plodding mule wagon. Then, too, a railroad would enable immigrants to flood
into western New York—and this would send the price of their

37

land soaring. A railroad would create new towns, new warehouse districts, new sources of supply, new markets. Prosperity would spread. Yes, they must have one of those railroad things.

Steins thudded in unison as the boisterous crowd resolved to stir up other communities to demand the New York assembly charter a stupendous rail line that would dwarf even the B&O's projected route from Baltimore to Wheeling on the Ohio. The New York rail system would run all the way from the Hudson River to Lake Erie—a mind-boggling 446 miles. What did it matter if none of the gentlemen drinking beer in Jones's tavern had seen a puffing locomotive or a freight car rattling into a station or even a line of rails. If Maryland was building one of those wonderful things, then, by durn, New York would have a better and longer one.

The Jamestown convention started things rolling. News of the resolution excited sentiments in other communities in the region. Within a couple of months enthusiastic representatives from nearly every county of the southern tier gathered at the village of Owego. Amid cheers and turmoil, Philip Church was selected to go to New York City to try to secure financial backing for a line to Lake Erie.

The odds were against Church, a rich former Englishman. Even his daughter-in-law found the idea of running a pair of rails over the chasm-clawed Alleghenies a little preposterous: "Mr. Church goes to New York for the winter," she wrote her father, "endeavoring to make interest for the railroad, which is now a topic of much feeling throughout the country. . . . They talk most seriously of being able to go from Buffalo to New York in twenty-four hours. You may smile at this, but I assure you, it's all true."

In New York City Philip Church was fortunate to have Eleazar Lord join forces with him. Lord was president of the Manhattan Fire Insurance Company and counted among his friends some of the wealthiest and most influential men in New York City. Church and Lord needed all the help they could get when they went to Albany, site of the New York legislature—for arrayed against them were the lobbyists of the powerful Erie Canal, who were determined to prevent the state from chartering the railroad. The Erie Canal men were concerned that the railroad would pirate away their trade. To help quell their fears Church and Lord proposed a route squeezed into the southernmost portion of New York. This concession helped, and the legislature granted a charter in April, 1832.

The charter stated that the New York and Erie Railroad Company (to use its formal name) could begin operating only after it had $100,000 in its treasury. Accordingly, stock was put on sale on July 9, 1833. Ten days later the Erie bank account had the required amount, and the stockholders were notified that an election for a board of directors would be held. Then the votes were counted and seventeen men were given direction of the company. The directors then chose Eleazar Lord to be president. The railroad was now ready to do business.

Lord's first task was to determine the exact route over which the tracks would be laid. There were numerous ways to get from the Hudson to Lake Erie. But some routes must cross steep mountains; some must span deep gorges; others must pass through regions where poor soil would restrict the future economic growth and thus the profitability of freight traffic. A well-conducted survey which combined the lowest mountains, the most gentle valleys, and the richest farmland was vital. For this a topnotch surveying company was necessary. But the Erie treasury, containing only a little more than $100,000, was pitifully inadequate to pay for a first-rate survey and still conduct the organization and promotion of the company.

Lord begged the New York assembly to finance the survey. After some haggling, New York reluctantly kicked in $15,000. The job was then awarded to Ben Wright & Co.

Wright divided the territory into two sections. The eastern one covered the most difficult terrain—the frowning Shawangunk Mountains just beyond Middletown and the awesome Starrucca chasm before Binghamton. The western section had its own problems though, what with the gigantic Lake Erie escarpment as well as the need to construct an entire port at Dunkirk on Lake Erie. Wright appointed division managers for each of the two sections, and they in turn organized a pair of field surveying teams to work under them.

The teams did the real foot-tramping. Each team was composed of around fifteen hardy souls. The head surveyor was a college-trained engineer. But his fellows could be about any young man who loved the outdoors. There was a head and a rear chain man, a man to hold the flags, someone to hold the level, a couple of men to map the region through which they passed, some teamsters to drive the three supply wagons, a cook and pot washer, and the inevitable dog, "for," as one surveyor declared, "a camp without one was, to us, the same as a home without children."

Life on a surveying team was one of hardship, vigor, and adventure. The areas which they investigated were largely unpopulated. The biggest "city" on the proposed route was Binghamton, with less than two thousand inhabitants. Goshen, another major center, had a roaring five hundred. Mostly there were fragrant woodlands, tumbling rivers, and blue-tinted, whale-back mountains. Primitive roads and horse trails meandered through the valleys, where farms sometimes hunched tiny shoulders into the primeval forests.

At night the surveyors pitched their tents on as level ground as they could. These tents were large canvas cabins, well staked to the earth, with a ditch dug around the sides to drain the frequent rainwater. The ditch diggings were piled around the tent bases to keep the wind out. There was usually a small iron stove inside, whose heat easily kept the tent cozy on even the most bitter night. The tent floor was composed of a foot or so of straw over which a wagon sheet was spread. When it was time for bed, the men tossed tarpaulins over the wagon sheet and blankets over the tarpaulins. The tents were really quite comfortable. and there was no question but that the surveyors had better quarters than the farm families in their drafty cabins.

When laying out the railroad route, the main concern was to keep the grade very low, for locomotives pulling heavy trains could not ascend steep grades. Indeed, the grade was usually less than twenty-five feet per quarter mile, so gradual that one could hardly see the change in altitude. It took precise use of surveyors' tools to determine the exact footage over a given route. To climb out of a valley or go up a mountain pass and still maintain a 2 percent grade or less, the surveyors had to plan routes that snaked back and forth across the slope, sometimes making wide horseshoe bends that would force the line to reverse itself for a mile or more.

The surveyors also had to bear in mind that a long train could not make sharp turns. This added to their difficulties in planning a low gradient, for there could be no hairpin curves up a mountain side. Neither could the route make quick turns to avoid a river chasm. It must bend easily—and when there was a chasm on the route, it must be bridged, not always at the most convenient point. Bridges were expensive, so the surveyors often routed the line several miles in the wrong direction to avoid bridging a stream.

Another problem that the surveyors had to consider was how far they should take the line away from the shortest route to Lake Erie in order to bring it to a particular town or village. If they tried to satisfy every burg howling for attention, the railroad would be shaped even more like a pretzel than it already was.

The surveyors looked like mangy backwoodsmen as they tramped over their assigned territory. Yet to the local inhabitants they were more like gods. They could make or break towns as well as individuals—for they were setting the course of the future. Where their transit stood on a forlorn flatland would one day be a handsome railroad depot with stores, warehouses, and a thriving town surrounding it. Where a red-tipped stake was driven into a swamp, there would one day be a long embankment cutting off a soon-to-die settlement from the surrounding farmland. For hundreds of years the route that the surveyors marked on their hand-drawn maps would remain almost as inviolate as the mountains themselves.

Early in 1835 Ben Wright presented the proposed route to the New York legislature. The lawmakers agreed that he and his men had done a good job squeezing the line far south out of canal country. Although the legislators grumbled about the two dips that the route took into Pennsylvania, they gave it their approval. The Erie was now ready at last to think about actual construction.

The first problem the Erie had to face was that of money. It was estimated it would take $5 million to complete the nearly 500-mile route—a far cry from the $100,000 in the Erie vault. Lord ordered the issuance of stock to try to obtain the construction funds, and quickly the directors began peddling the certificates to their wealthy friends in New York City. Investors snapped up the issue, and by the summer of 1835 subscriptions to $2.5 million worth of stock had been received. Not much of this was in cash, however, most being commitments for time payments. Nevertheless the Erie was now able to proceed with the first phase of construction.

The Erie ran ads in newspapers indicating that it would

accept bids for converting the route marked by surveyors' stakes into a broad, level roadbed. Construction was to start at the village of Deposit, some 200 miles inland from the Hudson. The first bids were taken for forty miles eastward. Out of the bids received, the Erie signed contracts with twenty-six separate companies.

The construction companies were very small. Each agreed to do the grading along less than two miles of right-of-way. They were to be paid around $8,000 per mile. For this meager sum—most of which they received in allotments as the grading passed certain points—each contractor had to hire his labor gangs and purchase innumerable wheelbarrows, picks, shovels, and rakes. He must also pay farmers with wagons and horse teams to haul the earth for his embankments and harrow the embankments into a gently graded roadbed over which rails could be laid at a later date. In addition, he had to secure freighters who would supply his crews with food, tents, and firewood. Then, too, he had to obtain a good supply of gunpowder for blasting through rocky obstructions. These expenses gnawed away rapidly at the small payments that the Erie doled out.

Yet work on the first forty miles progressed. Most of the laborers were big-fisted Irishmen, fresh from the immigrant ships that crowded into New York harbor. They would dig away at the hills of earth, load the dirt into wagons and wheelbarrows, dump it along the surveyors' route, and rake it level. For this grueling, morning-to-dusk work they received a whole 75¢—along with the cheapest slop food that the financially strapped contractor could obtain.

One day, amid the turmoil of grading, the contractors suffered a severe shock: the Erie was not able to pay their promised allotment. For the truth was that the Erie was out of money.

Rumor had long forecast this. Lord had been dismissed as

43

president, and Jim King had been placed at the helm. He had thought that he could meet Erie's debts by increased stock sales. But the Panic of 1837 had frightened investors out of the market. King had then gone to the New York legislature to beg for help. But many legislators were disenchanted with the idea of steam pots in general. One called the Erie "the greatest humbug of the age." The aid package that was finally passed had so many restrictions that it did the Erie no good at all.

And so work on the road stopped. The unpaid contractors angrily loaded their tools onto wagons. The Irish migrated back to New York City shanties. Weeds began to smother the gradings. The Erie Railroad seemed quite dead.

But the project would not die. The country was on the threshold of the railroad age. Forward-looking men were still thrilled by visions of great trains hurtling across immeasurable distances. The Erie was the nation's boldest project; when it was completed, it would be the longest railroad in the entire world. To permit such a project to die was like denying the nation its future. And so once again Erie advocates descended on the New York legislature. This time they got a good bill passed. New York would lend the Erie $100,000 to match each similar expenditure by the railroad—up to a total of $3 million. With this boon Erie stock sales were resumed. The road was abuilding once more.

Now the Erie began where it should have begun four years earlier—at the ends rather than in the middle. With Lord president again, Erie let out contracts for grading eastward from Dunkirk on Lake Erie and westward from Piermont on the Hudson River. Soon at Piermont a four-thousand-foot pier was constructed out into the Hudson. Here goods railroaded in from the interior could be shipped downstream to ready markets in New York City. At the same time nearby skilled stone cutters were fashioning quarry rocks into blocks that would support bridges to span the rivers that barred the way west.

In 1840 the entire 446 miles, except a rugged forty-mile stretch between Deposit and Binghamton, was under grading contract. By June, 1841, rails had actually been laid from Piermont fifteen miles west to the Ramapo Valley. A sturdy locomotive and some passenger cars were brought up the Hudson by steamboat and on the last day of the month half a hundred stockholders, reporters, and business leaders climbed aboard for the very first ride on the Erie.

It was a beautiful day. The passengers chugged along at fifteen miles an hour. Within a few minutes the Hudson was shimmering in the far distance behind them. Then the Ramapo Mountains loomed ahead. The rails skirted south of them through a dense forest. About an hour after starting, the excursion party reached the railhead at the hamlet of Ramapo. Almost everybody in town was there to greet them. Jeremiah Pierson led the passengers to his mansion, where food and drink were served in more than ample quantities. The trip back, made with the sun slanting over their shoulders, was as pleasant as the outward journey.

All the dignitaries knew that they were part of something big—something never before attempted. "It was a day which will be remembered when even the names of those who proposed this great work shall have been forgotten," was the way one journalist put it when he returned to New York City.

Grand as the excursion to Ramapo had been, the really gala celebration was reserved for the formal opening of regular passenger service in September, 1841. By this time rails had been laid as far as Goshen, some thirty-one miles beyond Ramapo.

At eight in the morning the Erie guests gathered at New York City's steamboat landing. The governor was there, as was the mayor. Other guests included a state senator, a bevy of

Congressmen, and virtually the entire New York City Council, as well as a host of eminent clergymen, business figures, and society celebrities. Two and a half hours later the steamboat had churned up the Hudson to the long Erie landing at Piermont. There the party was joined by author Washington Irving.

The two locomotives gathering steam at Piermont were among the most modern in the world. On these pacesetters the engineer and fireman no longer stood on an open platform. Instead there was an enclosed cabin to shelter them. Company officials explained that the two passenger cars were not large enough to hold all the guests—but why not ride in one of the open platform cars? It was a fine autumn day. In a festive mood, the guests gaily hopped aboard.

The speed was leisurely—only a little more than ten miles per hour. The passengers enjoyed the scenery, with the sumacs showing the first flush of scarlet. At first some guests were concerned because the flatcar decks pressed down upon the wheels, causing the wheels to saw into the wood flooring beneath them. But the sound of laughter and friendly chatter tended to drown out the wheel grinding, so everybody soon forgot about it entirely. Fortunately, the flooring did not fall apart, and the trip proceeded without incident.

By one that afternoon the trains had reached the picturesque meadows of Orange County. Farm families stood at the side of the railroad, staring open-mouthed at the first steam train some of them had ever seen. The dignitaries smiled at the rustics, but they too could not help but be awed by the miraculous invention that carried them along so effortlessly.

At two o'clock the trains puffed into Goshen. Several thousand persons had made their way to the little county seat. As the trains came to a stop, the village band broke into a boisterous, if somewhat dissonant, march. People cheered until their throats hurt. A few persons even fired guns into the air. Then

46

there followed several hours of speeches, with one orator declaring that the Erie would become America's Appian Way, a Highway of the Nations.

When the speeches were over, Major Edsall invited the passengers to his Occidental Hotel for feasting and drinking. The railroad people were in a jolly mood as they tumbled onto the platform cars toward sunset. By half past ten that evening they were back in New York City, hardly able to believe they had traveled nearly a hundred miles by locomotive in a single day at almost no personal discomfort. A horse and buggy could not have made half that distance, and a buggy trip would have left them jarred from toenail to scalplock.

Yes, truly a momentous age was upon them!

By the end of 1841 the Erie had four trains running on the forty-six-mile Piermont-to-Goshen section of the line. Two trains carried 250 passengers daily—the other two freighted some 100 tons of farm produce eastward and an equal amount of manufactured goods westward. The link between Piermont and New York City was completed by two company ships.

Despite the success of the showy but short Piermont to Goshen segment, the remaining 400 miles was in a state of disrepair and confusion. The open segment could not bring in nearly enough revenue to meet the Erie's construction bills. Company officials were unable to obtain more funds from the sale of stock and so the matching state contribution also dried up. In desperation the Erie appealed to New York for a loan. When the state refused, the Erie had no choice except to declare bankruptcy.

But numerous persons were determined to continue the ambitious project. The hundreds of creditors to whom the Erie owed money were persuaded not to force the sale of the Erie's equipment to help satisfy their accounts, for the locomotives, cars, and rails were worth only the merest fraction of what they were owed. Most of the money had been spent on grading, which was worthless until the railroad was completed.

A new president, Horatio Allen, was appointed in October of 1843. He found the company treasury so empty that not only had all construction stopped, but there was not even available the few pennies necessary to purchase office supplies. It was ridiculous. "We were building a railroad to cost millions," commented one director, "and we hadn't enough money to buy candles. There was positively not one cent in the treasury."

Yet the southern tier of New York counties remained strongly in favor of the line. The citizens of Middletown, ten miles west of Goshen, became so incensed because they could not secure a rail connection that they collected money from among themselves, sent a crew out to Dunkirk, ripped up the track laid at this distant western terminus, and hauled it back to Middletown. Then they relaid the track to Goshen themselves. That was one way to get the job done.

But a railroad could not be completed by feeding upon itself. President Allen could see no way out. Nor could his discouraged board of directors. All resigned late in 1844. In their place once more appeared the rugged Eleazar Lord, man of fierce energy and innumerable influential friends.

Lord burst like a volcano upon New York's financial community. By the use of newspaper ads and personal appearances he managed to lift $400,000 from the prickly pockets of New York City investors. Even more surprising, Lord collected three times that amount from the financially strapped southern tier. It was an indication of just how much they wanted the railroad.

With nearly $2 million in his coffers, Lord resumed work on the line. By December, 1844, he had looped his rails over the top of the wind-seared Shawangunk Mountains, and his grading reached to Port Jervis, twenty miles beyond Middletown.

Port Jervis was an important market town for a fertile section of Pennsylvania and New Jersey, as well as for New York. It was a valuable rail extension. But it was not enough. At twenty miles a year, it would take two decades to reach Lake Erie.

Lord needed more money. He had cajoled about all he could from private investors. So he turned to the New York legislature once more. Lord's artistic persuasiveness was at its best as he and his friends descended on Albany. Armed with the political power of the southern tier as well as the interests of many of New York City's financial barons, Lord was able to beat the canal and stagecoach blocs. On May 14, 1845, the state passed an act which enabled the railroad to issue $3 million worth of bonds. Not only that, but the state itself would sell these bonds to subscribers—on the condition that a track be completed from the Hudson to Dunkirk within six years.

The Erie was assured of the funds it needed. Now the task was to see if it could complete the rail by New York's deadline.

Eleazar Lord hoped he would have the glory of building the world's longest railroad. But it was not to be. Lord made some foolish routing decisions, and when he refused to alter them, he was forced out. Big Ben Loder, head of the opposition, took Lord's place in August, 1845. Loder was a giant of a man, heavy in body and thick in face. He did not fear great challenges—indeed, he believed they made life more enjoyable. One newspaper referred to him as the Hercules who would batter down the demons threatening the Erie. Yet even for a man of Loder's vigor, the going was tough. It wasn't until the final day of 1847 that the first locomotive reached the important junction of Port Jervis. By then two and a half years out of the six-year deadline had passed. And the struggling railroad had completed only seventy-four miles.

Nonetheless the Erie planned a great celebration to mark its entry into Port Jervis. Ben Loder and more than a hundred dignitaries took the train from Piermont. The guests could only gape with awe as the cars strained up the Shawangunks. The summit was reached via a fifty-foot-deep excavation through solid rock. Farther down the mountain they passed through a cut forty feet deep, extending nearly a mile in length. Even the most worldly guest gazed in admiration at the engineering skill—to say nothing of the impressive amount of human sweat involved.

In Port Jervis the passengers were entertained at Sam Truex's hotel. As the evening went on, wine flowed, and the celebration became ever more raucous. It ended with the party-goers smashing every piece of chinaware they could lay their hands on. When it was all over the next morning, the tavern looked like it had been hit by a dozen locomotives. Although the railroad had to pay $6,000 for the escapade, the stage had been set for the wild Erie "smashups," which marked the railroad's entry into other important towns on the line.

Loder now turned his attention to the next segment of the line—the difficult portion between Port Jervis and Binghamton. Although the Shawangunk Mountains had been bad, worse still was the thirty-mile gorge of the Delaware River just west of Port Jervis. In many places the rocks rose so steeply from the river that workmen could find no place to stand when placing their explosive charges. They had to be lowered in baskets. When the charge had been set and the fuse lighted, the blasters had to jerk frantically on the rope to be drawn up before the powder sent rocks hurling high in the air.

With great effort a ledge was blasted out of the Delaware rock. But matters did not become any better after the railroad left the Delaware at the village of Deposit. A dozen miles farther on it encountered the formidable Starrucca valley. To bring the rails down the steep valley side, then up the other wall, and still maintain a gentle grade would have necessitated an impossible length of track. Yet the alternative was also distasteful. That was to construct a 1,200-foot viaduct across the entire valley.

The viaduct was decided upon, and for an entire year nearly a thousand men labored at the project. Stone was hammered into blocks, and the blocks laid one upon the other until eighteen massive arches, some eleven stories high, reached in Roman grandeur across the valley. It was a masterpiece—America's greatest stone bridge by far. But it cost $1.3 million and left a gaping hole in the Erie's fast dwindling treasury.

There were more chasms to be spanned. Cascade Bridge, just a few miles east of the Starrucca Viaduct, was an intricate work of wood filagree—called by many among the Seven Wonders of the World. It was the longest single-span bridge in either hemisphere and soon became a major sightseer's goal. But the cost of the Cascade Bridge approached $100,000, so it too gnawed into the precious Erie reserve.

Nevertheless the railroad moved on. The grading crews made the roadbed level. After them came the gangs who put the wooden ties in place. Then hammers clanged as the rails were spiked into the crossties. Forward, ever forward the laborers moved. By the end of 1848 the spires of Binghamton were sighted.

Ben Loder had long awaited the moment when he could ride from Piermont to the central town of the southern tier. So Loder gave orders that his superintendents were to have two excursion trains ready to take him and a party of 400 to Binghamton. What did he care if it was December 26, in the depth of winter? What did he care if his guests boarded the trains at 4 A.M. in the midst of a swirling snowstorm? The men of Erie had never flinched in the face of the elements. Off to Binghamton they went.

Snow pelted the cars as they wound around the Ramapos. Goshen was little more than a gray outline, except for a knot of cheering citizens who looked more like snowmen than real persons. It was the same at Port Jervis. The Delaware canyon was eerie, with the wind screeching like a dozen steam whistles. The passengers huddled in their greatcoats, for the cars were cold and only half lighted by the lanterns, which swayed drunkenly.

It grew dark. The snowstorm increased. Yet the pair of locomotives chugged grimly down the throat of the gale. There was not a person aboard that was not impressed both with the reliability of the trains and with the heroics of the brawny men who had forged this road of rails from the resisting wilderness.

By eight that evening the first train puffed into Deposit. A welcoming committee was there to greet Loder and his guests. But Loder kept the ceremony brief, for Binghamton thirty miles farther west was his main goal. On they went into the frigid darkness. Over the magnificent Starrucca Viaduct and across the dizzying Cascade Bridge. Finally they saw the snow-softened lights of Binghamton.

The locomotives whistled loudly as they approached. They were answered by the roar of cannons. Quickly bonfires were lighted, making a Christmaslike entry to the depot. Here thousands of bundled persons had waited for hours in the fierce snow to see this wonder of wonders—a passenger train that had run the entire 200 miles from the Hudson River to Binghamton.

It would have been surprising if the celebration did not end in another Erie "smashup," although the accounts do not mention the casualties to Binghamton's crockery. But it was something to remember anyway, this eventful December 26, 1848.

The triumphant entry to Binghamton did not mean that the Erie was safely out of difficulties. Two hundred and forty-six more miles lay ahead before Dunkirk on Lake Erie would be reached. The state had granted the railroad only six years to complete the job, and this deadline would arrive on May 14, 1851. Loder was everywhere: in Dunkirk hurrying the segment of rail being laid eastward to meet the mainline; in Albany trying to keep the legislature from passing laws that would injure his railroad; in New York City and in the dozens of little towns on the railroad line desperately replenishing the funds that construction ate up like dry firewood.

In the middle of April, 1851, the great moment came: The last segment of rail was set on ties just east of Cuba Summit. Loder had completed the undertaking just thirty days before the state deadline. To celebrate, Loder, with his flair for the dramatic, planned an elaborate ceremony. He invited no less than the President of the United States to be his guest on the inaugural run of the first locomotive to speed between the Hudson and Lake Erie. Millard Fillmore accepted at once, as did his more famous Secretary of State, the incomparable Daniel Webster. So too did the Secretary of the Navy, two other cabinet ministers, the governor of New York, senators, representatives, mayors, bankers, businessmen, social leaders, and the aging Philip Church, who was at last going to take that railroad ride which his daughter-in-law had dismissed as impossible twenty years earlier.

The attention of the entire nation, as well as of much of the world, was on the Erie opening. It began in Washington, D.C., on May 12. 1851, when the President and his entourage boarded a train for New York City. Fillmore, Webster, and the others spent the night in Philadelphia, doing more entertaining than sleeping. The next day they were off on Charlie Frisbie's old line, the Camden and Amboy. At New York Bay they met Ben Loder and the Erie bunch waiting for them on a spanking new steamboat.

Loder took his guests across to New York City, where 50,000 enthusiastic persons, along with 9,000 smartly outfitted militia, thronged the Battery. Veterans of the Revolutionary War fired a salute. Many of them could recall the days not too long distant when the southern tier had not existed and a journey to the Iroquois-held interior of New York was a dangerous expedition not to be undertaken lightly. There were certainly some among the veterans who scratched their heads and wondered if America was not going soft with this modern easy rail travel.

After a gala evening in New York, the party took the steamer up the Hudson to Piermont, where the really exciting part of their journey was to begin. Loder had the landing decked with red, white, and blue bunting. As the steamer docked, a band broke into a brassy song, which was quickly obscured by the roar of cannons, the clamor of bells, and the cheers of onlookers. The guests then boarded the two trains, decorated with colorful banners from cowcatcher to rear platform. That is, everyone boarded except old Dan'l Webster. He wheedled Loder into providing him and his cronies with a private flatcar. From somewhere Webster secured a comfortable rocking chair. The weather was superb, Daniel said, and he preferred to view the scenery from the outside rather than from the confinement of a passenger car.

With Webster lounging in his big rocker, the engineers were given the signal to commence their epic journey.

The first segment was pretty much old hat for Loder and the Erie bunch. The trains dutifully stopped at Goshen, Middletown, and Port Jervis for speech making. There was a fine banquet at Narrowsburg along the Delaware River defile. During the afternoon the trains paused at the Cascade Bridge and the Starrucca Viaduct to allow the distinguished ladies and gentlemen to clamber over the rocks like school kids to gain good views of man's marvelous feats of construction. At Susquehanna, a major repair facility, sixteen locomotives were lined up on a siding to salute the company with whistles and bells. Late that afternoon the trains rolled into Binghamton.

The town was exuberant. Cannons popped. Bands tootled. Crowds yelped. But the town had had its proper smashup two years earlier, and Loder had other destinations in mind now. He held President Fillmore and Secretary Webster to a few minutes of oratory—which was nearly as difficult as building the Shawangunk cut. Then he sent his trains puffing west over gleaming rails that had never before pulsated to the wheels of a passenger express. The sun was copper-colored as they pulled into Owego, where the Erie concept had been born lo! those twenty years past. After a pause at Waverly, the trains halted for the night at Elmira (for the sleeping car had not yet been invented).

The party had covered nearly three hundred miles over rugged hills and across deep valleys. A horse wagon would have taken a week for such a grueling trek. But the railroad cars had glided over the distance in less than twelve hours— and the dignitaries had stopped often for food, drink, and palaver. Truly transportation had taken a quantum leap into the future.

Elmira had the customary plate-and-saucer smashup. But Fillmore, Webster, Loder, et al., held some of their energy in reserve—for tomorrow was the Big Day.

At six thirty the next morning, May 15, 1851, the trains moved out, with newly placed banners and bunting flashing in the dawn light. The crowds at Corning and Hornellsville were almost delirious as the steam monsters powered through town. Soon Cuba was passed, site of the final construction spike. Then the track was clear for the final run to Dunkirk.

There was a rush now to reach their destination. But the way was blocked at the hamlet of Allegany by Indians.

Although some braves were in warpaint, the days of red domination was a generation past. These Indians had gathered to gawk at the Great White Father, Millard Fillmore (who was president only because his predecessor, Zachary Taylor, had died in office). Smiling and hand shaking were Fillmore's strong points—and this he did with his usual dexterity. Then he proclaimed eternal friendship with the Iroquois. The Indians grunted something back. When the train pulled out, each group was pleased with the meeting. What did it matter if neither had understood a word of what the other had said?

Once the Indians were left in smoke and cinders, all eyes turned toward the west, scanning the horizon for the first glimpse of Lake Erie. At Dayton they saw it, blue and mirror-calm in the haze of fifteen miles. As the trains descended the high escarpment which separated the uplands from the Lake Erie basin, Loder's excitement grew. He well remembered making this trip on foot, stumbling over the briars, bushes, and broken promises of financial backers. Sometimes he had even doubted that the railroad would be built. Now here he was with the President of the United States and the venerable Daniel Webster about to ride handsomely into Dunkirk on an Erie train.

Loder's locomotives screamed out their arrival. From Dunkirk church chimes floated out to greet them. Then cannons from the U.S.S. *Michigan*, moored in Dunkirk harbor, boomed a presidential salute. The passengers could see that the water was speckled with steamboats and sailing vessels. The trains glided beneath a triumphant arch that welcomed them to Dunkirk. As the locomotives hissed to a stop, wild cheering broke out. It had been done—really had been done. From the Hudson to Lake Erie, 446 long, arduous miles. A journey of a week could now be accomplished in a matter of hours. The Erie was, as an official Citation of Merit from New York City would proclaim, "The Work of the Age."

That evening was the Erie's last and greatest smashup. A three-hundred-foot pavilion had been constructed for most of an entire block along Railroad Avenue. The banquet was magnificent: a pair of oxen barbecued whole, ten sheep roasted whole, boiled hams, and that most savory delicacy of all, smoked buffalo tongues. Steaming hot pork and beans were served in fifty-gallon tin pots. To soak up the gravy there were large sponges of bread cut from loaves ten feet long and so heavy it took two men to carry them. To wash it all down the guests dipped into large barrels of chilled cider that were spaced at intervals beside the table.

Ben Loder was called upon to make a speech, and of course he did. Millard Fillmore added his touch of homespun platitudes, and Webster spoke philosophical phrases that nobody understood. But the highlight of the evening was a speech by Peter Wilson, a full-blooded Iroquois who had been educated at Dartmouth. There was unconcealed admiration in the Iroquois' words, but they also contained an undertone of bewilderment that such a mechanical contrivance had invaded his ancient fatherland:

The paleface has completed a mighty work [Chief Wilson said]. He has overcome the most imposing natural barriers; he has pierced the valleys of the Delaware, Susquehanna, Chemung, Allegany, and levelled the hills which were roamed by my ancestors. Now their descendants marvel at the doings of the mighty paleface. They cannot but be pleased to see him accomplish his great destiny; to see him fly from hill to valley; and ride upon the wings of lightning.

There was deep irony in Wilson's words, for he could not have but realized that the railroad would forever alter the Indians' way of life. They had entered, whether they willed it or not, the era of steam. The mad dragons were upon them.

The following day the trains started back. The passengers

were exhausted by the festivities in Dunkirk. Most were quiet and reflective. As the forest slid past, garbed in May's transparent green, some of the riders realized that it was not only the Indians who were about to lose their time-old manner of living. American citizens from everywhere in the Union would find their independence lessening as bonds of iron drew them into a new economic system that would increasingly be dominated by large companies and big banking combines.

The Erie was the thunderhead of a new age. The "wings of lightning," to use the Iroquois phrase, were about to strike out across America. Life would never again be as it had been.

4

Empire on the Prairies

A lake steamer glided into a dock in the murky Chicago
River. Colonel Roswell Mason watched as the gangway
was hoisted into position. A frown may have wrinkled
the corners of his mouth as he surveyed the town into which he
was about to walk on this midspring day in 1851.

Chicago was a motley collection of mud-splattered taverns,
inns, shacks, and shanties. During rainy periods the entire
area from the mouth of the Chicago River clear out to the old
French portage, eleven miles southwest, was nothing more
than a vast swamp. Even the Indians had shunned the site,
which they called the *chicago*, or "bad smell."

However Colonel Mason was not repelled by the rather
dismal habitation of 40,000 rambunctious persons—indeed,
twenty years later he would become its mayor. The colonel saw
the place as a challenge—and he had never disdained challenges. Hadn't he been instrumental in building the famed
Erie Canal? He had also extended his engineering talents into
railroading, where he was a prime mover in the Housatonic

Railroad and, in quick succesion, the New York and New Haven lines. Now he was about to start the greatest undertaking of his already eventful life—construction of the Illinois Central Railroad.

Illinois had had very poor luck with its railroads. The original Central Railroad had been chartered back in 1836—only six years after Peter Cooper's contraption had opened the railroad age. The plan was to have the Central build down the state from north to south. Four other railroads were to cross Illinois from east to west, intersecting the Central at favored locations quarter distances through the state.

It was quite ridiculous for the underpopulated frontier state to plan for 1,300 miles of track when the Erie would have difficulty laying just 446 miles through a far wealthier and much more populated area. Illinois' overly ambitious scheme had dragged to its foreordained conclusion a few years later. By then more than a million dollars had been squandered, and the state was hopelessly in debt. All that had resulted was a few miles of track that went nowhere and one squeaky locomotive rusting in the prairie.

Stephen Douglas, Illinois' fireball senator, got the project moving again in 1850 when the Senate considered his bill for a new Central Railroad. Douglas' bill was brilliant. The federal government owned thousands of acres in Illinois that were virtually worthless because there was no access to them. Douglas proposed to give a railroad company a small portion of this land—alternate sections in a band twelve miles wide along the proposed route. These land grants would provide a tremendous reserve against which the railroad could borrow—and, as the railroad was built and access to the land was gained, the sections, which were a mile wide on each side, could be divided into quarter sections of 160 acres each and sold to settlers. Thus the land grants would almost guarantee the success of the railroad. They would, at the same time, ensure that the remaining land, which belonged to the government, could be sold. By this means Congress would receive millions of dollars without taking any risks or doing any work. What could be easier? Douglas asked.

Despite the bill's merits, Congressmen debated it furiously, for the idea of giving away federal land stuck in many throats. Finally the bill became law, and the nation's first land-grant railway was authorized. The Illinois Central Railroad Company received a formal charter from the State of Illinois on February 10, 1851.

As Colonel Mason descended the gangplank which led to a crude boardwalk that ran along the Chicago River, he undoubtedly mused over the charter. It allowed the Illinois Central barely four years to complete the main line, which would extend 300 miles from Cairo in the south to LaSalle on the Illinois River. Not only that, the Illinois Central was to have two branches off the main line. One would connect with Chicago on Lake Michigan and the other with Galena near the Mississippi River. This would bring the total mileage to 705 and must be completed in two more years. Thus the IC must build nearly 60 percent more track than the Erie and yet take only six years compared with Erie's eighteen. Even though the IC had no Appalachians to obstruct construction, the task was formidable.

Colonel Mason scratched his chin whiskers. Imagine, in just six years the IC must survey the routes, construct the gradings, build the bridges, and put up the depots. It must somehow obtain the rails from British foundries and the ties from remote Michigan and Wisconsin forests. And there was the problem of obtaining laborers, for Illinois was a virtually unpopulated state. Farmers, too, must be lured into this vacant country, since the IC would be dependent for income not only from farmers' purchases of IC land but from the freight and passenger service farmers would pay for once they were established along the railroad.

The colonel grinned. It was a quite impossible task. But it would be done.

Within just two days after reaching Chicago, Mason and his staff had organized their surveying parties. Each was to cover around 100 miles of the proposed route. As with the Erie crews, Mason's surveyors had to consider the streams to cross, the hills to surmount, the embankments to be built—and make the route not vary more than seventeen miles from the most direct route—that was in the charter.

The surveying parties that set out from Chicago by horse, mule, and wagon during May of 1851 found that the actual surveying was not difficult. The forested hills of southern Illinois did not approach the ruggedness of the mountains the Erie had to cross—and the prairies of central and northern Illinois, well. they were softly rolling grasslands with no steep inclines, few rivers of any size, and not even any trees to obstruct rail laying. By September the survey pegs had been staked out, and maps were drawn showing the exact route of the main line and the two branches.

The surveyors' only real problem concerned the railroad's entry into Chicago. The most logical way would have been along the South Branch of the Chicago River to the station of the four-year-old Galena & Chicago Union Railroad (now the Chicago & Northwestern), Chicago's first railroad. But the Rock Island Railroad, which had just started building, owned land that obstructed the IC's most favored route. So the IC surveyors were forced to plan their line along five miles of Lake Michigan waterfront, ending at the mouth of the Chicago River, where a terminal must be built separate from that of the G&C.

Chicagoans were delighted by this development. Stephen Douglas made a bundle of money when he sold a block of his lake-front property to the IC. As for the Chicago City Council, its members had worried for years about the encroachment of the lake against the fashionable homes close to the water. Therefore the IC was granted the lake-front route only on the condition that it construct a breakwater. This long breakwater, together with the immense wooden trestle that was to support the IC tracks above the lake's crashing waves, was an expense the IC directors had not planned on. Yet when the trestle was at last completed, it would provide the IC with what became known the world over as the most magnificent entrance to a major city. Some claimed the number of persons who traveled the IC just to ride the lake-front trestle eventually paid for the structure with their fares.

Construction work on the IC line began in 1852. The first problem, just as predicted, was obtaining laborers. Colonel Mason was frantic. "I do not believe there is one-fourth enough men to do the work now under contract," he complained. "My only hope is a large emigration from the East."

Mason did more than just hope for workers. He actively pursued them. Illinois Central agents met immigrant boats docking at New York and New Orleans. Soon Germans, Poles, Danes, and other Europeans were taking advantage of the cheap transportation to Illinois offered by the IC agents. Mason even sent his hawkers as far as Ireland, where 1,000 men were induced to migrate to this exotic corner of the New World to work for the fantastic rate of ten cents an hour.

The labor crews soon found that Illinois was far from the paradise that IC leaflets pictured it to be. The main difficulties were encountered in the prairie section that encompassed the northern and central portions of the state. Never had Europeans experienced anything like it. A crew building south from Chicago or LaSalle would spend weeks engulfed in a world of grass. It was a weird, unnerving experience, this Illinois grassland. "For miles and miles," one observor wrote, "we saw nothing but a vast expanse of what I can compare to nothing else but the ocean itself." The grass billowed and swayed with the wind like breakers rolling in from some vast distance. Yet there was no crash or roar, only an eerie hissing as grass fronds scraped endlessly against one another. Grass was everywhere. Once in a while the survey pegs led the construction gangs to a tiny grove of trees, rising like a blessed atoll in a green Pacific. But the grove was eventually left behind, and once again there was no object to break the awesome monotony of grass.

The prairie was more than uneasily haunting. It actively worked against the laborers—just as if it knew the coming of the steel rails would spell its doom. The thick grass roots clutched the moisture of spring, and the scrambled ridges prevented the water from draining. As the gangs dug the railroad embankments, mud oozed constantly about them. But worse than the mud was the danger of cholera, which came from microbes thriving in the stagnant water. Cholera was a horrible sickness which resulted in painful muscle cramps, followed, after twelve agonizing hours, by death. Men hard at work one day would be dead the next. In one camp 200 of the 1,600 inhabitants died of cholera. The disease took the lives of countless workmen, who were buried in unmarked graves beside the tracks.

Colonel Mason worked fiercely to replenish his dwindling labor supply. Over a period of years he brought more than 100,000 men into the state for railroad work—although he rarely had as many as 10,000 in his camps at one time. Yet somehow he kept the work going. One group built south from Chicago, one north from Cairo, and one in both directions from LaSalle,which was kept supplied from Chicago by the newly opened Illinois and Michigan Canal. Month by month the rails moved forward. The schedule was being met. Illinois would have its long-awaited Central Railroad.

Local citizens of quick wit and sharp business sense soon began making plans to take advantage of the changes the railroad would bring. Such was one Daniel Brush, who left us a little book entitled *Growing up with Southern Illinois.*

Dan had watched carefully to discover the exact location of the rails. Even before the surveyors reached his portion of Illinois, he made plans to tramp into the forested wilderness to discover the exact route the railroad would take. He felt certain that the hamlets of DeSoto and Makanda would become railroad stations. But there was a space between them with no settlement. If he could just find some logical place where the railroad could be expected to locate a station—and if he could purchase a great deal of land on this site—why then he might well have his fortune made.

About the first of August, 1852 [Brush wrote], accompanied by Asgill Conner, I commenced my search on horseback, and came to a small improvement in this vicinity owned by John Brewster. Here we were compelled to leave our horses and pick our way as best we could through a dense mass of vines, briars, and tangled underbrush until we found the line of the railroad—a path which was cleared of luxuriant growth. By the grade stakes we could see the line of survey as well as the profile of the road. By following the line and carefully noting the numbers on the stakes, we discovered that for about one mile, through parts of sections 16 and 21, the roadbed would be level.

This flat site was nearly on a direct line between Murphysboro and Marion, Brush discovered as he held up his map. Both towns were county seats. Brush let out a whoop. He had it! Although the area now was bleak and desolate, he was confident that the railroad would convert it into a populated place. The next thing to do was obtain control of the land.

That was impossible for Brush to do alone, for he simply lacked the funds. Therefore he nosed his horse down to Jonesboro, headquarters of the railroad crowd. In Jonesboro he looked up Lew Ashley, IC construction chief for southern Illinois. Ashley had some buddies who were ready to join Brush and plunk money down on the site once Brush described it to them. In August, 1852, twelve of them got together and drew up an agreement binding them to the project. Brush suggested that, because their prospective town was located in a coal region, it be called Carbondale. The others concurred. Then each of the dozen paid $100 into the treasury, for which they received individual company certificates. Now they were ready to move ahead on their risky real-estate gamble.

Nine hundred of the $1,200 that had been collected from the twelve stockholders was used to obtain 360 acres (at $2.50 per acre)—two thirds of which was sold by the government, which held the portion of the odd-numbered section that the townsite occupied, and a third promised by the IC, which held the portion of the even-numbered section.

Once in possession of the land, the stockholders drew a plan of the townsite and divided it into lots. Some of the lots were small and in the town's center; these were meant for stores and businesses. Others were larger and farther out; these were designed for private homes and gardens. A central square of more than 60 acres was reserved for the railroad company—and this information was quickly mailed to the IC bigwigs in Chicago, who, it was hoped, would see that here was a place for warehouses, switchyards, and a handsome depot. To keep the town an attractive place for families, Brush and his fellow speculators set aside four lots for churches while, at the same time, agreeing not to sell lots to tavern keepers. Half of all the lots were given to the stockholders, which they could either hold in reserve or sell at whatever raise in price they felt they could obtain. The rest were kept by the company and made ready for public auction.

Now the company had a town—on paper. It had wide streets—but no carriages ran down them. It had lots for homes and businesses—but no houses or stores had been built on them. It had church grounds—from which no spires rose. It had a fine expanse of acreage for railroad use—but no trains hooted and no track glistened. Brush had sunk nearly all his liquid assets into a backwoods desolation, and all he had was his still worthless stock certificates and the dreams conjured by a row of puny surveyors' stakes.

In December, 1852, Brush began work on a small log cabin, only six paces wide and the same across. He stocked it with some goods from his store in Murphysboro and officially opened it for business on a chilly morning on New Year's Day, 1853. Brush's sales could not have amounted to much that day, for in all of Carbondale there was only one tiny house belonging to a stockholder's relative, and one other structure, the property of Brush's friend, Asgill Conner. Carbondale's first minister gave a sermon in Conner's place, which had only a floor, a roof, and a quartet of end posts with no walls between.

Four days later Brush and his company had the audacity to offer the first lots for sale. Incredible as it might seem, a goodly number of persons made the difficult trek through the thorns to reach Carbondale—such was the lure of being on a possible railroad switching site.

Dan Brush and his fellow stockholders watched nervously while the lots were auctioned off. Although they varied greatly in size, the average lot may have been around an acre, for which Brush paid $2.50. But, as the bids began, the price paid rose to $6.00. Soon a buying fever caught the crowd. Choice lots near the railroad preserve went for $50 to $60 each. One man even paid an astounding $100 for a single lot. And this while no one even knew for sure that the IC would not just shoot the trains on to DeSoto or Makanda without stopping at the place called Carbondale.

But Brush, and now many others, were confident that Carbondale had a future. Using the profit from his land sales, Brush built a sawmill in a ravine just outside the town's limits—for he knew that the IC, gradually building northward from Cairo, would need wood for railroad ties, engine fuel, and depots. Brush was busy on his sawmill when the big news came, and it was even more encouraging than he had dared to hope. The IC had decreed that the strategically situated townsite would not only have its very own passenger station, but that it would be given a switchyard for handling freight. Furthermore, the IC planned to build a freight house in Carbondale. And when the time came to award the contract, it was given to the only person in Carbondale with a sawmill and lumber. And, that, of course, was none other than—Daniel Brush.

Throughout 1853 the town began filling. The new settlers could talk of nothing else except the coming of the railroad. They were isolated now, but the railroad would change all this. In place of mud roads that kept a wagon moving slower than a lame dog, the steel rails would enable locomotives to whisk farm goods off to a market with unbelievable quickness—even in rain or snow. In anticipation of the day the trains came to town, Brush erected a good-sized general store. Then, at the IC's request. he constructed a storehouse for engine firewood.

In the early part of 1854, like a slowly rising tide, the IC began seeping into Carbondale. One day, from the far southern distance, someone heard the faint whistle of a locomotive as it carried rails and timber to the gangs that were digging the embankments, doing the grading, and laying the track. A few days later a train whistle was heard from the north, for other crews were working down from Centralia. The progress was slow, since the Shawnee Hills were a nasty barrier and the Big Muddy River required bridging. But each day the whistles grew a little louder. Whenever they sang through the trees, the townsfolk stopped what they were doing to hear the music the whistles made. Excitement was beginning to build.

One evening the first construction men stomped into Carbondale, for it was now easier to wagon to this town than take a handcar along the tracks to DeSoto or Makanda. The crews were made up of tough hombres. But Brush and his townspeople had kept the whiskey parlors out, so the more riotous of the railroadmen went other places for their redeye. Those who remained in staid Carbondale behaved themselves—and bought armfuls of goods at Brush's general store.

It wasn't much later that the Illinois Central supply wagons began making regular calls on Carbondale merchants for supplies. Money started flowing into the town. As Brush wrote, "prosperity abounded."

There was frenzy in the air during June, 1854, as it was realized that the IC planned to reach Carbondale on the Fourth of July. What a celebration it would be, marking both the seventy-eighth anniversary of American Independence and the arrival of the fabulous railroad! The glorious occasion demanded more than just an outing for the inhabitants of the growing little town. The whole world—or at least all of southern Illinois—must be part of it. And so invitations were sent to all the surrounding metropolises: Jonesboro, Anna, Murphysboro, even mighty Cairo down on the Ohio River.

As the acceptances flowed in, the people of Carbondale set out to make the celebration one worthy of the occasion. The height of the festivities would be a banquet no one would ever forget. Women all over town began baking bread, making cakes, cooking poultry. The men barbecued great legs of beef. Farmers carted in vegetables from fields that had not existed a year earlier. And as they worked, they looked up to see grading crews leveling the earth on Carbondale's outskirts—and behind them, tie men lowering massive railroad planks on the grading. "The scream of the fiery demon was heard in his approaches from the south," Brush wrote with his usual rainbowed prose. Then came the moment when the tracks were pounded down right through the town itself. But the locomotives remained spouting flames a quarter mile away. Their entry to Carbondale was reserved for the Fourth.

At last the holiday was upon them. Throughout the morning families arrived in wagons and on horseback and on foot. Men, women, children, dogs—in they poured until the streets were dense with an excited, milling throng. Few had ever seen a railroad. They touched the tracks and jumped along the ties, then quickly jumped off. For there was something a little fearsome about these magical things that were about to change their lives.

The sun was high and the fever hot when the moment approached. The crowd hushed as the rumble of the locomotive was heard:

Then came the shrill cry of the steam whistle [Brush wrote], and soon the locomotive and cars slowed up and came to a stop opposite the freight house. The wonderstruck people shouted, some in terror and all in surprise. The horses cavorted and tried to break away. The dogs howled and, with tails tucked between their legs, made hasty strides towards tall timber. . . . Then the startled multitude, perceiving that no one was hurt, quieted down. A Fourth of July oration was pronounced in a grove near the station under a Union banner that I had purchased for the occasion. . . .

After the speeches, came the sumptuous feast. There were 3,000 persons in all—a massive crowd for this backwoods region. By evening they had all gorged themselves on Carbondale's delectables. Then Brush led them to the freight house. He told them to stay there in front, for he had something wonderful with which to top off the day. Walking several hundred feet down the gleaming tracks, he opened boxes of fireworks which he had bought especially for the event.

Brush sent his first rocket swooshing up into the July darkness. As it burst into flaming sparks, the crowd gasped in awe, for not one in a hundred of them had ever seen such a sight. More rockets flared above the IC freight house. Greens, blues, oranges, silvers, and flashing reds—the sky seemed to be on fire. When Brush lighted his Roman candles, more brilliant geysers of color burst forth, lighting the railroad ties for a quarter mile.

It all climaxed with the Grand Finale—more grand than Brush himself had planned, for one rocket did not perform exactly as it should:

It fizzed and fluttered, and instead of ascending into outer darkness, as a well behaved skyrocket should have done, it gyrated around sometimes up a little and again down, and finally ended its course by tumbling, fire-end foremost, right into the open box containing the residue of my works. The fuses took fire, and then the fun started in earnest. . . . The rockets began to hiss up the street. They started squirming and jumping this way and that and, seeming to sight the dogs, took after

71

them up the hill and into the bushes, wriggling streaks of fire. . . . The magic wheels rolled and tumbled, the Roman candles shot forth the best they could, the crackers all popped at once, and the torpedoes with loud reports exploded.

The crowd, thinking this was an ordinary part of a fireworks display, yelled with delight. When the last torpedo had exploded and the last rocket zipped off in search of dogs, there was a stunned silence followed by a round of wild applause for Brush. "The crowd, then, dispersed," Brush recalled, "rejoicing and jubilant, contented with the past and sanguine of prosperity in the future. There was a whoop for Carbondale and a hurrah for Illinois and its first big railroad. The 'Good Time' seemed close at hand."

It was like this in most of the towns springing into life along the newly laid IC tracks. Never had there been anything like it. One year the state was a virtual wilderness, and a few years later it abounded with towns and smiling farmlands. Some towns soon had their own colleges, and a few such as Carbondale and Champaign eventually converted these colleges into true universities. Many townsfolk became wealthy and influential, as did Daniel Brush, who developed into a grain wholesaler, a banker, and a respected church elder.

The population of Illinois soared—particularly along the IC route. In 1820 the state had barely 30,000 persons, almost all of them living in the southern tip of the state, where communication with the rest of the world was by way of the Ohio and Mississippi Rivers. Chicago did not exist, except as a trader's hut or two, a dilapidated government frontier fort, and a campsite for miscellaneous bands of roving Indians. By the time the last rail was laid at the appropriately named town of

Mason in 1856, Chicago was a boomtown with 109,000 fast-buck inhabitants. The rest of Illinois was also partaking in the population surge, with the counties along the IC boasting 800,000 persons. By this time the fame of the IC, as the longest, most dynamic railroad in the world, was known on both sides of the Atlantic.

The amazing influx of people was not entirely due to the natural appeal of the Prairie State. From the very beginning the IC directors were aware that they had to hurry settlement, since the railroad was dependent on land sales to obtain construction and operating funds. Therefore the directors appointed an agent to run a high-powered promotional campaign to advertise the bounty of Illinois. The most vigorous of the agents-in-chief was John Wilson. Under his guidance, the IC became a dominant factor in the settlement of Illinois.

In promoting the state—and, in particular, the land along the IC—Wilson encountered certain problems. Illinois had something of a bad reputation for outbreaks of cholera and for the difficulty of plowing the tough prairie sod. In addition, Illinois was viewed as a poorly run state, since it was refusing to pay interest on the bonds issued a few years earlier for the first Central Railroad. Yet cholera was now well under control, Illinois was making plans to resume interest payments, and a new steel plow being produced by John Deere in Moline, Illinois, could slice readily through the fibrous matting of grass roots that had mocked the old wooden plows. Wilson knew that if he could get the true facts to those leather-skinned men and women who toiled the overworked eastern and southern farms, he could create an instant mass migration to Illinois, with its thick, black, virgin loam.

And so Wilson's agents fanned out through the nation. They attended county fairs, spoke in public meetings, plastered IC posters wherever there was a wall—or any flat surface. "The great Illinois Central Railroad," commented a

Memphis newspaper, "with ten thousand placards . . . stuck in every hotel, barroom, steamboat, and barbershop, in all colors and shapes . . . is making more noise at present than perhaps any other road in the Union." IC ads blossomed in just about every newspaper in the nation. "Illinois, the Garden State of America," the ads blazoned. "The Finest Farm Lands—Equal to Any in the World!!!"

Who could resist Illinois after reading Wilson's ballyhoo? "No State in the Valley of the Mississippi offers so great an inducement to settlers. . . ." Wilson's posters ran. "There is no part of the world where all the conditions of climate and soil so combine to produce corn and wheat. . . . The great resources of the State . . . are almost untouched. . . . They await the arrival of enterprising and energetic men. . . ."

The promotional campaign worked. The settlers came by train over the Erie and connecting rails to Chicago—by flatboat and steamboat down the Ohio—by horseback and mule wagon over the National Road. They came by the thousands to settle mainly in quarter sections of land close to the vital IC tracks. The IC made everything possible—and profitable—this was the sentiment of John Williams in 1855:

When I first settled in Vermilion County, we had no market for any of our produce; we had no railroads. . . . Times have changed indeed. . . . Instead of 5 to 8 cents a bushel for corn, we now get 25 to 40 cents; and in place of spending some four days getting to Chicago we now go up on the morning [train], do our trading, and get back home the next day.

All along the IC route the new farmers and their families were part of the fantastic bonanza that the IC had started. Between

1850 and 1860 the wealth of Illinois multiplied five times, and the area under cultivation increased by 300 percent.

The fame of Illinois spread even to Europe—helped, it must be admitted. by Wilson's far-ranging agents. Norway and Sweden were crisscrossed by an IC man who distributed pamphlets, wrote newspaper articles, and talked with Scandinavian farmers at any hamlet where he could gather an audience. In Germany, too, an IC agent was active, and he headed the German Land Company, which was in effect an overseas branch of the Illinois Central.

The railroad charter had decreed that the IC could not sell any of the even-numbered sections which the government had donated to it until Uncle Sam had disposed of all his odd-numbered sections six miles on each side of the tracks. Government land went quickly at $2.50 per acre, and soon there was only IC land left. The IC sold its land at an average of $10 per acre—thereby gaining a fabulous cash flow into its treasury. Thus, even from the beginning, the IC had none of the serious financial worries which had plagued (and was continuing to plague) the Erie Railroad. Obviously the land-grant system was a vital element in a railroad's success. Nearly every line built after the IC would benefit by the IC's example and receive government land grants.

The wealth of the IC did not mean that its service could be called luxurious. A passenger boarding the train found himself in a cramped, narrow car usually jammed with up to fifty persons. His seat was hard backed—as well as hard bottomed. As he tried to wiggle himself into a moderately comfortable position, the engine would start with a jerk which might send his hat toppling onto the seat behind him. If the weather was hot, he might grunt up the always-sticky side window. Should he manage to get the window open, he would probably be greeted by a cloud of sooty smoke in the face—unless his car was far enough in the rear to receive merely a pelting rain of cinders.

Summer was bad enough. But winter was worse. Then no one dared open the windows, and a half hundred men, women, and children sat hunched together, soggy, steamy, and sweaty from heat radiating out of the pot-bellied stove, which simmered cherry red at the far end of the aisle. There was no effective way of regulating the stove heat—either it blazed or it died. Once in a while, when the train lurched over a bad section of track, the stove would topple over. Then the hot coals would tumble down the aisle like fire beetles. The passengers would leap onto the seats to avoid the coals, while the conductors and a few male volunteers snatched them with metal tongs before the car went up in a blaze.

After a journey of many hours, a passenger might want to relieve his cramped position by walking around. This was a futile wish, for there was simply no place to go. The aisles were always heaped with travel bags and squalling children. It was strictly forbidden to move from one car to another while the train was in motion, for the primitive link-and-pin coupling resulted in a great deal of slack between cars, and this in turn caused a jerking that had sent more than one person hurtling right over the side. Then, too, the coupling had an unfortunate tendency to break apart. Thus it was not too uncommon for the head of the train to chug merrily on down the track while the rear portion ground to a slow, infuriating halt.

Slumped in his ever-hardening wooden seat, a passenger had no choice except to endure the ordeal. The motion of the train itself was far from comforting. In many places the IC, in order to meet the building deadline set by the state, had laid the tracks right over the prairie sod—paying little attention, for the time being, to a level roadbed or an adequate foundation for the ties. To riders traveling over such a roadbed the experience must have been much like that editor Horace Greeley had on an 1859 rail journey through Missouri: "It was raining pitilessly for the second day nearly throughout," Greeley wrote, "so that the roadbed was a causeway of ooze, into which the passing train pressed the ties, first on one side, then on the other, making the track as bad as track could be.... It afforded more exercise to the mile than any other railroad I ever traveled."

What with the swaying roadbed, the sharp bumps of the track joints, the jerks of the couplings, and bounce of the car springs the passengers were jarred, jostled, and jolted for most of their journey. Knowing this, it is surprising that some passengers would prefer sleeping on the trains to a night in a relatively comfortable hotel. But evidently the demand was there, for by the mid-1850's crude sleepers were in use on the IC and other lines. The railroad executives, with good reason, doubted that their sleepers would be very popular, for the first of them were stubby little half-cars with just two series of upper and lower berths on each side. At both ends of the car was a tiny closet in which there was a tin washbasin, a drinking can with a common cup, and a toilet which opened onto the tracks (which meant that one had to resist nature's call when the train was in a station).

The sleeping berths were far from comfortable. There was a lower berth. which rested on the floor, and an upper, which was secured by ropes halfway down poles running from the ceiling. The passenger would climb into his berth and there, behind a heavy curtain which shut off both light and ventilation, attempt to sleep. Of course he would go to bed with his clothes on, for bedding did not include sheets. All in all a night on an early sleeper, with "the noise, the shaking, the dust, the stifling atmosphere, and the nauseous smell" (as one contemporary described it) was not among the most sought-after experiences.

Passengers found that the railroad did not do much better with regards to his eating accommodations. There were no dining cars as yet, for the frightful bumping and swaying would have caused the food to bobble onto passengers' laps. Instead, the IC provided eating places (they could hardly be graced with the term "restaurants") at three stops along the Chicago to Cairo run—which took around sixteen hours. It was a long journey, and the passengers would glance at their pocket watches while their stomachs growled. At last Champaign, Mattoon, or Centralia would slowly materialize out of the boundless prairies. As the train wheezed to a halt, the passengers would leap from the cars and dash to the eating area of the station. The counterman and his wife were almost overwhelmed by the sudden crowd. Nevertheless, they somehow managed to shovel out their ready-cut ham slices, hard-boiled eggs, bread loaves, pies, cakes, and coffee. The passengers would wolf down the grub and shout for more. It was a madhouse of yelling, munching, snorting, and slurping. And there were always a few who were still stuffing their mouths as the departure whistle shrieked. They would hurry out, still chewing, and catch the handrail of the moving train at the last possible moment.

Between skirmishes at the food counters, passengers could enjoy—if that's the right word—stale snacks that young boys called news butchers peddled aboard the trains. Although the news butchers made most of their meager earnings from selling daily papers, they were glad enough to offer their captive audiences such delicacies as dusty candy, soggy peanuts, and last week's glazed popcorn. When someone did not quite finish his repast, the news butcher would collect what remained after the passenger left, dump it into another container, and resell it on his next run. Even with all this careful harboring of his resources, the young teenager often had to resort to the ancient art of short-changing to gain what he regarded as his proper wage. Yet not all the news butchers shared these shifty morals. Twelve-year-old Tom Edison, one day to illuminate the world, worked as a news butcher on a railroad out of Detroit in 1859. Edison's grateful patrons received hot bread, fresh butter, and home-grown vegetables which Tom bargained for at stops along the way.

Whatever the shortcomings of passenger service, the Illinois Central attracted an ever-growing clientele, and soon railroad officials began looking beyond the state's borders for even more business. Large numbers of immigrants from Scandinavia and Germany were traveling to Minnesota, North and South Dakota, and upper Wisconsin. In order to capture a lion's share of these onrushing pioneers, the IC built a large wharf and terminal at East Dubuque on the Mississippi River. From there the IC made connection with a fleet of nineteen fine steamboats sailing upriver to the newly opening areas. And, as these lands evolved into prosperous farms, grain began to flow downstream to Dunleith, where it was stored in a huge IC grain elevator prior to being transported by freight train to the East.

The IC also turned its attention to the South. During the 1850's it built its own steamboats to link Cairo, its southernmost terminus, with Memphis, Vicksburg, and New Orleans. The Illinois Central steamboats were among the largest and finest on the Mississippi. On them Chicago pork and ham went south, and Delta cotton came north.

Soon the IC was making plans for a magnificent railroad empire which would encompass the American heartland from the chill borders of Canada to the steamy tidewaters along the Gulf of Mexico. Rails would replace the steamboats as soon as possible. A start was even made for a bridge to span the

Mississippi at Dunleith, and from there for rails to reach far out into Iowa. By the end of the 1850's the IC was serving eight states and was fast becoming a dominant force for the development of the interior. It was, in the words of Senator Stephen Douglas, "one of the most gigantic enterprises of the age."

5

The War Trains

I t was a bleak day in February, 1861. Abraham Lincoln stood in the gray drizzle, tall and gaunt, his deep, melancholy eyes scanning the faces of the people who crowded around the rear platform of his railroad car. The locomotive had its steam up, and clouds of dirty smoke hung above the squat brick depot at Springfield, Illinois.

Standing pensively before them, Lincoln thought about the momentous task which would confront him when he took the oath of the presidency in a few weeks. He wondered at his audacity in seeking an office with such awful responsibilities. Even now seven Deep South states were meeting in Montgomery, Alabama, to establish the Confederate States of America. Lincoln loved the Southerners as if they were kin—hadn't he himself been born in Kentucky, a slave state? Yet he couldn't permit them to break up the Union, which was a sacred beacon of freedom and democracy to a dark world downtrodden by despotism.

As Lincoln stood on the railroad-car platform, he may have

considered the military potential of the two sections. If he had, he would certainly have taken heart from the North's superior railroad system, which bound the upper Mississippi states to the East. In just the past ten years, rails had been completed between New York City and Chicago, Philadelphia and St. Louis, Baltimore and Cincinnati. Nearly a dozen feeder lines ran down from the major cities to points on the Ohio and Potomac Rivers. Troops could be moved along them with a rapidity that would revolutionize military transportation. So, too, could guns, ammunition, and all the other vital matériel of war.

The eastern Confederacy, on the other hand, had only two railroads running across its territory, and from Atlanta to the Mississippi there was only one. Thus the North was on fast-moving wheels, while the South was still largely on foot or horseback.

Lincoln roused himself from his reverie. "My friends," he told the thousand or so gathered around him, "no one, not in my situation, can appreciate my feeling of sadness at this parting.... I now leave, not knowing when, or whether ever, I may return." He spoke for a few moments more before ending with "an affectionate farewell." Then the engineer pulled the whistle, and a minute later the locomotive's drive wheels began to turn. Bells in Springfield rang as the train moved majestically out of town.

Lincoln watched the countryside whirl past. Soon he was out of Illinois and into Indiana. Railroads were still newfangled inventions to most persons. But to him they were nearly as familiar as the stovepipe hat in which he had carried his notes when he was a lawyer on the circuit. He had been involved with the Illinois Central from the day of its inception—indeed, as a young lawmaker, he had been influential in securing the IC its original charter from the State of Illinois. Later he had done considerable legal work for the IC—and a juicy $5,000 fee had enabled him to finance the debates with Stephen A. Douglas that had been his springboard to the presidency.

Lincoln knew that the railroads would not only change warfare, but they would alter politics. He was one of the first politicians to take advantage of the new mobility that the rails made possible. In going to Washington he decided to take a series of railroad routes that zigzagged across the Northern states, thereby enabling him to see the people and confer with state leaders.

Lincoln moved in a stately, if somewhat erratic, procession to Washington. His first major stop was in Indianapolis. Next he visited Cincinnati and from there angled up to Columbus, Ohio. Then he headed to Cleveland, Buffalo, Rochester, Albany, and on down the Hudson River line to New York City. After considerable pomp and ceremony in New York, Lincoln took the train south through Trenton, Philadelphia, and Baltimore, to arrive in Washington twelve days after he left Springfield.

On March 4, 1861, protected by rifle squads on the surrounding roofs, Abraham Lincoln was inaugurated. A little more than a month later Jeff Davis ordered the bombardment of Fort Sumter at the entrance to Charleston harbor. General Beauregard's first shells splintered against Sumter's walls, and the Civil War began.

Almost instantly the value of the railroads became apparent. In July, 1861, Lincoln sent General Irvin McDowell marching on Richmond, the Confederate capital, with a hastily trained army. McDowell had thirty thousand men and expected a rather easy victory over Beauregard, who opposed him with only twenty-two thousand at the village of Manassas, a junction on the railroad to Richmond. But just before the battle Confederate troops from Joseph E. Johnston's army in the Shenandoah Valley, sixty miles west, began to arrive by way of a railroad which ran over the mountains. All day the Shenandoah trains ran a shuttle service. By afternoon the Confederate forces had swelled to thirty-two thousand, and a counter-charge drove McDowell back across Bull Run Creek. Thereupon the Union army fled to Washington in utter demoralization.

The crucial role played by a railroad at the first battle of Bull Run was not lost on Union war planners. Northern strategy centered on attacking the Confederacy's sea and land transportation. While the Federal navy began to close Southern ports to the importation of foreign manufactured goods, upon which the section was so dependent, Federal armies were mobilized to sever the South's internal transportation.

The Mississippi River was one major objective, with the citadels of Vicksburg and New Orleans the key points to be taken. But the Mississippi, after all, ran north and south. What was really vital was the east-west movement of troops and matériel. In this matter two railroads played essential roles. One was the Memphis and Charleston, which, in combination with other lines, ran the entire width of the South from the Mississippi to Virginia. The other was the Western and Atlantic, which connected Atlanta with both Richmond and Memphis.

In the drive on the M&C, the Illinois Central played an important part. Cairo, the railhead on the Ohio River, became a major supply depot and training camp as the railroad carried in recruits from all over the Midwest. These men were disciplined into soldiers, and on February 16, 1862, a spearhead under Ulysses S. Grant captured Fort Donelson, the Confederates' key bastion in western Tennessee. As the troops in gray fell back southward, the way was open for Grant's advance on the Memphis and Charleston Railroad, particularly the rail hub of Corinth, Mississippi.

To ensure that the M&C was cut, Lincoln hurled a second

army into central Tennessee. Just as Grant was supplied by the Illinois Central, Don Carlos Buell, commanding the Army of the Cumberland, was supplied by the railroad which ran through Louisville, on to Cincinnati, and then fanned out in a series of independent lines all over Ohio, Indiana, and Michigan. Buell's drive was even more dangerous than Grant's, for should he capture Chattanooga, he would cut the M&C and, at the same time, be poised against the Western and Atlantic.

When Buell took Nashville in the spring of 1862, the Richmond government became greatly concerned. The Memphis and Charleston Railroad was "the vertebrae of the Confederacy," declared General L. P. Walker, former Secretary of War. And the current war secretary, Judah Benjamin, wrote to Robert E. Lee that the M&C "must be defended at all hazards." Rebel troops were removed from the seaboard and hurried west. Additional troops were taken from New Orleans, even though the city was under the threat of an imminent Federal attack.

At Nashville Buell conferred with a Union spy named Jim Andrews. Andrews had traveled many times on the vital 140-mile Western and Atlantic Railroad between Atlanta and Chattanooga. He had conceived a plan, based on his knowledge of the W&A, to help the North win the war. It was not only spectacular, but actually workable. As he outlined it to Buell, Andrews' idea was to lead a small band of men posing as Southerners to Marietta, twenty miles north of Atlanta. Then, as Buell was marching against Huntsville, Alabama, on the Memphis and Charleston Railroad, Andrews and his raiders would capture a W&A locomotive and speed northward, burning every bridge on the W&A. This would make it impossible for the Confederates to send reinforcements to the defenders at Huntsville. Once Huntsville had fallen, Buell could capture Chattanooga and from there move down the W&A on Atlanta itself.

85

Don Carlos Buell listened to Andrews with skepticism. He did not think highly of the scheme—there were too many elements left to chance. Besides, Buell, a spit-and-polish military man, did not care personally for Andrews with his splotched clothing, frazzled beard, and wild eyes.

Although Buell dismissed the scheme as impractical, General Ormsby Mitchel (who had once been a railroad surveyor and knew the value of rails) did not. Mitchel, commanding one of Buell's divisions, was impatient to bring his 10,000 troops into action. Therefore he permitted Andrews to recruit twenty-three men from his force. And it was decided that on the morning of April 11, 1862, Mitchel would attack Huntsville while, at the same moment, Andrews and his raiders would commandeer a Confederate locomotive and destroy the W&A bridges.

On the cold, damp evening of April 7, Andrews and his men gathered in a secluded cove just south of Nashville. As Andrews spoke. lightning flashed behind him. "You'll break up in small squads of two, three, or four," he told them (according to Billy Pittenger, one of his men). They would travel on foot south to Chattanooga, which Andrews gave them three days to reach. From there they would take the W&A train to Marietta, reaching it the night of the tenth. The next morning they would nab their locomotive, and the thrills would begin.

The men were excited. Each had been handpicked by Andrews for resourcefulness and love of adventure. "This was glorious," Pittenger said for all. "The thought of returning into our camp after piercing the heart of the Confederacy set every nerve on fire." They would be heroes.

And so they set out into the night.

Chattanooga was 102 miles ahead of them, and ordinarily they could have made it in the allotted time. But constant rain had turned the roads into pasty quagmires. Sloshing ahead was painfully slow—so that it was not until the evening of the eleventh, rather than the tenth as Andrews' plans called for, that the men finally assembled at Chattanooga. They were a day late now. It could be serious, as each of them was aware.

While they were awaiting the train for Atlanta the next morning, telegraphs buzzed the fateful news that General Mitchel had taken Huntsville. Instantly Chattanooga was in an uproar. The depot was suddenly crammed with persons wanting to flee from the hated Yankee army. Nevertheless, Andrews and his men were able to elbow their way through the people to board the train.

As they chugged toward Atlanta, the men noted the eleven railroad bridges over Chickamauga Creek, as well as the great span at Resaca. If these bridges could be burned tomorrow, the railroad would be useless for days. Mitchel could take Chattanooga long before reinforcements could be rushed up from Atlanta. Yet, at the same time, the men were shaken by the number of trains on the single track line. Tomorrow, when they would be streaking north, they would have to pause at turnouts for many more southbound trains than were normal. Would this allow pursuers to catch them? It was a question that worried many.

They spent the night in a Marietta hotel crowded with Chattanooga refugees. After a fitful sleep, the raiders were up at dawn. When the train from Atlanta pulled in, they saw that it was drawn by a locomotive called the *General*—one of the fastest in the South.

Andrews and his men boarded the forward passenger car in small groups, thereby escaping scrutiny by quick-tempered Bill Fuller, the twenty-six-year-old train conductor. The whistle sounded shrilly as the engineer, Tony Murphy, pulled the throttle. Murphy was an experienced train driver, having worked for several years on the Erie. Eight miles ahead was the Big Shanty station, where Andrews intended to make his move. One hundred and twelve miles farther north was Chattanooga, and in between the eleven vulnerable bridges that spanned its approaches.

As the train slowed for Big Shanty, the raiders gripped their pistols. At Big Shanty, in the shadow of massive Kennesaw Mountain, the raiders were dismayed to find the station alive with Confederate soldiers, for Big Shanty had become a major training camp for troops to be sent by rail to battle Buell and Grant. But the camp was on the west side of the tracks. Therefore Andrews decided to capture the locomotive by moving in from the east.

Big Shanty was a breakfast stop. Since no one dreamed there was the slightest danger from Yankees here in the heart of the Confederacy, no guard was posted on the train. Even Fuller and Murphy went to the diner. When the train was almost vacant, Andrews walked leisurely to the locomotive. Seeing it was empty, he had two men climb into the cab while another pulled the coupling pin that disconnected the locomotive and three empty boxcars from the rest of the train. "Back at the door of our car [Billy Pittenger recalled] Andrews spoke in his ordinary tone, not a whit louder or more hurried than usual. 'Come on, boys,' he said. 'It's time to go now.' Our hearts gave a great bound, but we rose quietly and followed him." The raiders sauntered along the east side of the train, then hopped into the rear boxcar. A Confederate sentry stood not twelve feet away, idly watching them. Once they were in the boxcar, Andrews returned to the locomotive and nodded to Bill Knight, experienced engineer from Ohio. Knight drew the throttle. As the sentry's eyes opened with astonishment, the locomotive and its three boxcars slowly moved north, leaving the rest of the train standing on the tracks.

Fuller and Murphy in the diner gasped as they saw their engine chug out of the station without them. Shouting angrily, they dashed outside. When the locomotive continued despite their shouts, the two railroadmen ran up the tracks in pursuit—as the soldiers howled in laughter at the absurdity of chasing a locomotive on foot. But Fuller and Murphy knew no alternative, for Big Shanty had no telegraph station, and if the locomotive was to be somehow stopped, it was up to them to do it.

A couple of miles beyond Big Shanty, Andrews stopped. While some men blocked the tracks behind them with logs, Johnny Scott scrambled up a telegraph pole and hacksawed through the cable. Andrews was jubilant. "When we've passed one more train," he told them, "the coast will be all clear for burning the bridges and running on through to Chattanooga and around it on the spur track. For once, boys, we've got the upper hand of the Rebels!"

Andrews had Knight run the locomotive at a slow speed, for he did not wish to arouse suspicions by going faster than the regular train would have done. Besides, there was little likelihood of pursuit from behind. Just to make certain, however, he paused outside Acworth to lift out a rail—which took five minutes of intense crowbar pressure to release the spikes. The raiders then dumped the rail onto the floor of a boxcar and hauled it off as they continued their unhurried progress north. Now there was no chance whatsoever that a locomotive could catch them from the rear, for there was no way one could get over the gap in the rails.

But Fuller and Murphy had not given up. They had come upon a handcar and were pushing it by means of a pole up the tracks after the raiders. At Acworth they picked up a pair of double-barreled shotguns, which would put them at an advantage over the raiders who were armed only with short-range pistols—if they should ever catch up with them. The track gap caught them by surprise, and their handcar ca-

89

reened off the track and overturned. But it was a simple matter to right the light little vehicle and carry it to where the rails began again. And so they were soon off once more.

Fuller and Murphy eventually reached Etowah, where, to their surprise and delight, they discovered a freight engine on a siding with steam up. Breathlessly they told the train attendants about the hijacking of their locomotive. The astonished freight men had never heard of such a thing, but they knew Fuller and Murphy and, after a few moments of debate, lent them their locomotive. The pair leaped aboard and rammed the throttle wide open. The locomotive roared into life. The chase was on!

Meanwhile Andrews, keeping his slow pace, had reached Kingston. Here a problem developed. The southbound train from Chattanooga had not passed down the one-way track yet, so Andrews was forced to cool his heels on a siding. But when the train at last puffed into the station, the engineer told the stationmaster that Andrews should not proceed because a second train was following, carrying refugees fleeing from General Mitchel's army. Andrews' men, who were hidden in the boxcars, waited tensely for the second train to arrive. But when it finally pulled in, the engineer announced that yet a third train was behind it.

This was too much for Andrews. He exploded to the stationmaster that his boxcars were filled with ammunition essential for General Beauregard. Then he boldly demanded that the switches be set for him to move onto the main track. Although the stationmaster was horrified that Andrews would dare run his locomotive up the track in the face of an oncoming train, he was convinced by Andrews' forceful manner that Beauregard's ammunition demanded certain risks. So the switches were set, and Knight started the *General* up the track.

Four minutes after the *General* left Kingston, Fuller and

Murphy roared into the station. Everyone was thoroughly aroused when they were told that Andrews was a fraud. With angry shouts, dozens of armed men leaped onto Fuller's freight train. Off they sped. But just when it seemed as if they would catch the Yankees, they spotted a place where the track had been ripped out. As the freighter screeched to a stop, Fuller and Murphy yelled for the others to follow on foot. But the unruly men simply lounged around the stalled locomotive, cursing the Yankees and popping off their guns. They ridiculed Fuller and Murphy for continuing the chase on foot. Nevertheless, the pair had come this far and were determined to go on by whatever means were at hand. So they quickstepped up the tracks and soon left the others in the distance.

Luck was again with Fuller and Murphy. They had not gone far before they came upon Pete Bracken, running his locomotive on a siding. His engine was none other than the *Texas*, one of the few locomotives that could rival the *General* in speed. When they told Pete what had happened, he motioned for them to board. Then Bracken let out the throttle and began high-balling northward. The great train race was on again.

Andrews knew nothing of what was happening to his rear. His main worry was the train that was bearing down on him from Chattanooga. He decided to drive pellmell for the switch-out at Calhoun, hoping to make it before colliding with the other train. Knight gave the throttle full power. Billy Pittenger, riding with the rest of the men in one of the boxcars, was jerked about as the speed picked up. "We had no hope of stopping in time if the belated passenger train should be met," Billy recalled. "We might as easily have reversed a cannon ball in flight. If the passenger train started out from Calhoun before we came in sight, it was almost inevitable death for all our party."

Everyone on board was chilled by the speed. No locomotive

had ever gone this fast. Alf Wilson, throwing wood into the fire that raged in the boiler, could hardly believe their whirlwind velocity:

It was frightful to see how the powerful iron monster under us would leap forward under the revolutions of her great drive wheels. Over and over, Brown would scream at me, "Give her more wood, Alf!" The locomotive rocked and reeled like a drunken man, while we tumbled from side to side like grains of popcorn in a hot frying pan.

It was bewildering to look at the ground, or objects on the roadside. A constant stream of fire ran from the rims of the great wheels. We sped past houses and fields and out of sight, almost like a meteor, while the bystanders, who barely caught a glimpse of us as we passed, looked on in both fear and amazement. It has always been a wonder with me that our locomotive and cars kept on the track at all.

Andrews, who timed them with a watch, calculated their speed at seventy-two miles an hour—and this on a track with the rails not well spiked and over a roadbed built for twenty m.p.h. Knight blew his whistle constantly, hoping the other engineer would hear it and stop. Behind him Fuller, Murphy, and Bracken were racing equally fast on the *Texas*. They caught Andrews' whistle and knew they were keeping stride with the unsuspecting raiders.

As Andrews began slowing for the Calhoun station, he spotted the passenger train just pulling out. The Chattanooga brakemen brought the passenger train to a halt, then the engineer frantically backed up in time for a switchman to send Andrews' locomotive onto the station siding. Had the passenger train left Calhoun just sixty seconds sooner, Pittenger believed, it could never have stopped in time.

The engineer was boiling mad and would not permit Andrews to leave the siding, which his long train was blocking. Finally, in desperation, Andrews gave him preemptory orders, using as his authority General Beauregard himself. After a moment of indecision, the engineer moved his cars forward, and Andrews let out his throttle.

Hardly had Andrews disappeared than Murphy, Fuller, and Bracken rumbled into Calhoun—rousing the fury of the passenger engineer, for this stretch of railroad was supposed to have been kept clear for him. But when Fuller and Murphy explained the situation, all was changed. As they roared off, the passenger engineer joined the chase—as did eleven regular soldiers who hopped on board a tender locomotive.

Andrews still had no idea that Confederates were so close. In front of him lay open track—no more southbound trains to delay him. The Resaca bridge was just ahead, and once that was aflame, the rest would be just a joy ride. To make absolutely certain, however, that there would be no one to interfere with the bridge burning, Andrews stopped to remove another section of rails.

To pull the spikes out was slow work, for they had only one crowbar. As each crosstie was loosened, some of the men loaded it into a boxcar, for they would need the crosstie wood to burn the bridges that were soaked after a solid week of rain. The iron rail had just been loosened to the point where, if all the men pushed, it could be bent far enough to disrupt the track. Then occurred the moment Billy Pittenger would remember forever: "At that instant, loud and clear from the south, came the whistle of the engine in pursuit. By the sound, it was near and closing in fast. A thousand thunderclaps couldn't have startled us more." A second later the *Texas* hove into view. With that the raiders stopped trying to bend the rail and dashed back to the *General*. Andrews opened throttle for the Resaca bridge.

As Andrews sped up the track, his men punched a hole in the rear boxcar and began tossing ties onto the track as a barrier to the Confederates. With the bridge rapidly approaching, Andrews had to make an important decision. Although the bridge was covered with a wooden roof, the timber was thoroughly wet, as were the crossties and kindling with which they hoped to make a fire. If their pursuers should come upon them while they were trying to get the timbers to burn, they could warn the Resaca stationmaster just beyond the bridge with whistle shrieks. The stationmaster could then toss wooden barricades across the tracks, and the raiders would be trapped. Therefore, with great reluctance, Andrews decided he did not have time to burn the bridge. Instead, he uncoupled one of the boxcars and left it in the bridge darkness—hoping the train behind would crash into it. Then he resumed his flight northward.

Fuller, Murphy, Bracken, and five companions they had picked up en route had to stop many times to remove the ties thrown onto the tracks. But they knew the raiders would eventually run out of ties. Soon they saw the Resaca bridge. Slowing down, they coupled with the boxcar Andrews had left. Then they picked up speed. "From the instant we got over the bridge at Resaca," Fuller said, "the race became one for life or death between the two engines, both five-feet-ten-inch drive wheels, with 160 pounds of steam, and throttles wide open. No such race has ever been run, either before or since." And somewhere behind Fuller and Murphy was the train carrying the ten soldiers—and behind them was the passenger train that Andrews had encountered at Calhoun. Each of the three pursuing trains was running in reverse, since there were no turntables to set them right. Onlookers gaped in disbelief as first Andrews, with his boxcars broken at the end, then the three reverse-running trains hurled past at breakneck speeds.

At one point Andrews stopped, uncoupled another of his boxcars, and shoved it back toward the Texas. But Bracken skillfully reversed his direction in time to couple on with the car. Then he resumed his forward speed, later leaving the boxcar on a siding.

As the race continued, Andrews discovered that he was running out of firewood. He realized he must get more or the game would be up.

When we reached Green's woodyard, there was no lingering in the work of loading up [Pittenger wrote]. The wood was piled in frantically by men working for their lives. But before we had half filled the tender, we again heard our relentless follower. So eager were we to get the largest possible supply of fuel that we didn't take their first whistle as a sufficient warning to start. . . . The enemy, seeing our engine standing, was actually obliged to begin braking to avoid the collision that seemed inevitable.

Even so Andrews did not get a full load. As the Confederates opened up with their muskets, he was forced to abandon the woodpile—accompanied by catcalls from the Confederates, who, according to one of the raiders, "were worked up to an infuriated pitch of excitement." By dumping some of the logs they had just obtained on the tracks, the raiders began to outdistance the rebels. Shortly they saw the Dalton station. Ramming through the covered depot at full speed, they sent men, women, and children scurrying for cover. They had to trust to luck that the switches had been set right. Knight, at the throttle, saw to his horror that the track seemed to terminate at the end of the depot. He shut his eyes as he waited for the fatal wreck. But at the last moment the track made a sharp curve to the left, and the *General* blasted out from under the depot roof into the countryside.

Bracken kept right on their trail, as reckless as Knight. Both trains thundered over the rails, their wheels flashing sparks. They barreled through Tunnel Hill, where Pittenger and many of the others urged Andrews to stop and ambush the rebels, for the *General* was again just about out of fuel. But Andrews shouted to them that they were almost at the first of the Chickamauga bridges and still had a chance. Andrews then ordered his men to rip the boxcar sides into kindling and set the floor afire. As they thundered northward, rain pelted them, and it was only with great effort that the kindling was made to flame.

At last the first bridge was reached. Andrews had his brakemen stop halfway through. It was a large structure protected by a wooden roof and wooden sides. They threw almost all their remaining wood fuel onto the boxcar fire. Slowly the flames rose to lick the wet rafters. But there was no time to build a good fire, for the hated rebel train appeared down the track. Andrews reluctantly moved out of the bridge. Hardly had he left than Bracken pushed the smoldering boxcar to a siding.

Andrews now was down to his last fire logs. Alf Wilson, the fireman, remembered how the end came:

The locomotive shook and reeled as she sped on. I could liken her condition to nothing else than the last struggles of a faithful horse whose heartless master has driven and lashed him until he is gasping for breath and literally dying in the harness. The powerful machine had carried us safely for almost a hundred miles, some of the time at a rate of speed appalling to contem-

plate, but she was becoming helpless and useless in our
service. She was shaken loose in every joint, at least she
seemed so; the brass on her axles and boxes was melted
by the heat; her great steel tires were almost redhot,
while she smoked and sizzled at every joint.

They had almost succeeded. Had they been a day earlier
with no southbound trains to delay them, they could have
done it. Had Murphy and Fuller not been so persistent against
apparently hopeless odds, they could have done it. Had the
day been sunny rather than one of ceaseless rain, they could
have done it. Had Bracken been driving any locomotive than
the speedy *Texas*, they could have done it. Even now they were
tantalizingly close to the Chattanooga bypass, which might
have enabled them to meet Mitchel's army marching east from
Huntsville. It had been close—very close. But it was all over
now. For the *General* was down to its last few logs.

"Jump off and scatter!" Andrews shouted. "Make it to the
loyal states as best you can." Raiders began leaping from the
boxcar and locomotive. When no one was left except Andrews
and Knight, Andrews had his engineer stop the engine, then
reverse it against their pursuers. Having played their last card,
the two men jumped off and headed in different directions
through the woods. Bracken reversed his engine and made
gradual contact with the abandoned *General*. The great train
chase was over.

Not only did Andrews' raiders fail to wreck the W&A Railroad, but General Mitchel did not take Chattanooga. He battled to the very outskirts, and even erected batteries across the
river. But reinforcements failed to arrive, and eventually he
had to fall back. As for the raiders, most of them were captured by the Confederates. Andrews and seven others were

hanged. But the rest, including Billy Pittenger, the group historian, were soon back in Union territory as the result of a prisoner exchange.

The idea of taking Chattanooga and striking down the W&A was not given up, however. Toward the end of 1862 General William Rosecrans, who had succeeded Buell, moved toward the city. But it was not until September of the following year that he occupied it. The door was now opened for the drive down the W&A to Atlanta, vital junction of four important railroads and a rallying point for the entire Deep South. The tough job was given to William Tecumseh Sherman.

The March on Atlanta was the crucial campaign of the entire war. The fight for Richmond received more attention, but Richmond was in the far corner of the Confederacy. Atlanta was in its heart. Richmond could fall, and the South would still be whole. But if Atlanta fell, the Confederacy would be split and its transportation system completely smashed. General Joe Johnston was ordered to hold Atlanta at all costs. Although Johnston had only 60,000 troops to Sherman's 90,000, Johnston's men could fight from behind earthwork protection, whereas the Federal troops would have to charge across open fields. Since attackers customarily needed a two- or even three-to-one superiority against entrenched defenders, Johnston believed he had more than enough soldiers to protect Atlanta.

In May, 1864, Sherman began moving down the W&A Railroad. Extending behind him was a vast array of locomotives and railroad cars loaded with war goods. Sherman's railroad supply line reached to Nashville, which had been turned into a huge complex of warehouses and quartermaster tents. From Nashville the supply line continued to distribution points on the Illinois Central, the Wabash line, the Baltimore and Ohio, and a score of lesser Midwestern railroads. Ninety thousand men would eat a lot of food, wear out a lot of uniforms, use up a lot of gunpowder. Freight trains were running throughout the Midwest to keep Sherman supplied.

Johnston dug in at Dalton to await the Federals. But Sherman had no desire to throw his men against Johnston's maze of earthworks. So he sent part of his army off to the right in a double-time half loop that brought it to Resaca, ten miles behind Johnston. Resaca linked Johnston to his own supply line, which ran down the W&A to Atlanta. But Sherman's detachment lacked the power to cut the line, for Johnston's guards at Resaca stoutly held them off until Johnston could pull his main army out of Dalton.

Slowly during the spring Sherman moved down the strategic railroad. He never risked an outright assault, for his army was not large enough to absorb the frightful losses such an attack would cost. Whenever Johnston dug in, Sherman would send a flanking force swinging around the Confederate lines to threaten the railroad. Then Johnston would have to retreat without a major fight. Gradually the blue wave moved into Calhoun, then Kingston—where Andrews and his men had spent an agonizing hour waiting for the Chattanooga trains.

By the end of June Sherman had reached Kennesaw Mountain and the Big Shanty station. The Confederate training camp of Andrews' day was gone now, replaced by a network of entrenchments and gun ports that made the mountain a Gibraltar of Rebel strength. Sherman unwisely abandoned his flanking tactic and ordered a frontal assault. After losing 3,000 men unnecessarily, he resumed his flanking movement. Johnston was forced to abandon his impregnable Kennesaw fortifications on July 9 as Sherman bypassed him. Jeff Davis angrily replaced Johnston with John Hood. Hood was ordered to fight, not retreat. At the battles of Peach Tree Creek and Ezra Church, Hood managed to keep Sherman from entering Atlanta. Therefore Sherman again utilized his brilliant railroad tactics, as throughout August he had his men gradually extend a cordon around the city to cut the four railroads by which Atlanta was supplied. Hood now realized what Johnston had understood long before—that his army needed the railroads more than it needed even Atlanta itself. Hood reluctantly abandoned the city and on September 2, 1864, the pride of the Confederacy was Sherman's.

Now Hood decided to play Sherman's game. Knowing that he lacked the force to meet Sherman on open ground, Hood moved north to strike the railroad upon which he supposed Sherman to be dependent. However, Sherman refused to panic. He sent 30,000 troops back to join with other Union forces in combating Hood. Then, after burning Atlanta to the ground, Sherman did an incredible thing. He marched his remaining 60,000 men not north along the W&A but southeast—deeper into Georgia. In doing so he not only cut himself off from supplies but from telegraph communication with Grant and Lincoln, his superiors in Washington. No one in the North knew where Sherman was. It was as if he had simply been swallowed up by the South. When questioned, Lincoln himself admitted, "We know where he went in, but I can't tell where he will come out."

Had one studied a map of Southern railroads, he could pretty well have guessed where Sherman would emerge. He was simply following the Georgia Central Railroad to Savannah. Of course, after Sherman passed down the line, the railroad was no more, for its complete destruction was the primary reason for his famous 250-mile March to the Sea.

As Sherman's men trooped through Georgia, they were impressed by the results of Federal attacks on Southern transportation. While Confederate troops at the front went hungry, central Georgia was bursting with fat hogs, meaty potatoes, and fruits of all kinds. The problem was that there was no efficient way to transport all this bounty to the front.

Sherman had counted on Georgia's granaries being full, since his only food was to come from levies on the plantations through which he passed. In this he was not disappointed.

Sherman rolled into Savannah after a month's march. There he and his men were resupplied with uniforms and ammunition by Federal ships. Then Sherman was off once more—and again he followed the railroad. Southern strategists reasoned he would strike hated Charleston, birthplace of secession. But to Sherman Charleston was a mere gadfly. His primary goal was to destroy the railroads. So he left the Confederate army waiting for him at Charleston and hit straight north to take Columbia, the capital of South Carolina—and, vastly more important, General Robert E. Lee's best source of supply. Once Columbia fell, Lee's troops defending Richmond were increasingly hard pressed for war necessities.

Sherman's objective was to wreck the South's ability to supply her troops. With this in mind, everywhere he marched he burned buildings and destroyed railroads. Joe Johnston, back in command of the Confederate forces opposing him, could mark Sherman's progress by the smoke that followed him.

On up the railroad Sherman plunged, a juggernaut of flaming fury. He crossed into North Carolina, his men chanting "John Brown's Body" as if they were the voices of God Himself. The death knell of the Confederacy was being sounded as Sherman ripped up its railroads.

While Sherman was devastating the Deep South, Grant was poised before Lee's grim troops entrenched at Richmond. For four long years the Confederacy's capital had been the goal of Lincoln's eastern armies. Although Grant had not managed to blast Lee out of the city, he had extended his lines so that he was just outside Petersburg, the rail junction through which Richmond's supplies flowed. On April 1, 1865, Grant mounted a furious assault—and Petersburg was taken.

Jefferson Davis was at church the next morning. The sky was clear as spring water. The Confederate president felt good, for rumor had it that Lee had crushed Grant's assault in a surprise attack. But halfway through the service a messenger hurried down the aisle. He stopped before President Davis, breathing hard, and handed him a note. Davis turned pale as he read it. Grant could never take Richmond—but he had taken Petersburg. Without rail connections Richmond could not be held.

The Confederate army tramped dejectedly out of Richmond. Lee intended to take his defeated force south to join Johnston. But in his heart he knew it was hopeless. He had lost rail communication with the rest of the Confederacy—Sherman had seen to that. His men had almost no food or ammunition. And they desperately needed fresh reinforcements. But there was nowhere to get them in a hurry, for the rails were closed.

Lee and his men made it as far as the village of Appomattox Court House, about a hundred miles west of Richmond. Then Grant caught up to them. With Northern railroads furnishing the Union armies with everything they needed, Grant's superiority was so overwhelming that further resistance was futile. On April 9, 1865, Lee surrendered.

The world's first railroad war was over.

6

The New World of Transcontinental Travel

T he train whistle echoed loudly among the wooden buildings of Omaha. The engine gave a great chug, then another, and then a third. Slowly the drive wheels turned. Passengers saw dust and cinders rise before their windows. They felt a quickening throb as the train burst out of the depot and into the sunshine. For a few moments they watched Omaha's stores and homes flick past. Then the town was gone, and they were on the Great Plains.

The train was long, with a baggage car up behind the coal car and a series of passenger vehicles and sleepers behind. In the very rear was the super-fancy Pullman Palace Car. On this morning in April, 1877, the Pullman was occupied by the famous publisher Frank Leslie, his beautiful wife Miriam, and a dozen or so artists, writers, and photographers—all friends or employees of Leslie.

It was a high-living group. Leslie was one of the nation's premier publishers. He had a joy of life, as reflected in such of his magazines as *The Jolly Joker, The Chatterbox,* and *The Comic*

Almanac. Vivacious, golden-haired Miriam was either the King of Belgium's love child or a onetime circus rider from New Orleans—take your pick. She was as witty and gay as her husband was robust and free-spending. Now, together with their sparkling associates, they were on a cross-country excursion, the luxury of which typifies railroading at its finest.

Although they had set out nine days earlier from New York (to a society "bon voyage" complete with fireworks), there had been nothing sensational about touring the East. Railroad travel was common there by this time. But west of Omaha—ah, there was adventure. For the nation's first transcontinental railroad, linking Omaha with San Francisco, had been completed in 1869—just eight years earlier. So new was travel in the West that Frank Leslie was certain a firsthand account of such a trip would boost the circulation of his most famous publication, *Leslie's Illustrated Newspaper.*

"With Omaha behind we leave the last suggestions of life in the States," wrote correspondent Brace Hemying for Leslie's readers. "Our road lies west on the straight single track of the Union Pacific." The train moved at a steady twenty miles an hour—five times faster than the horse-drawn farmers' wagons that it rushed past. The ride was smooth in the hand-crafted Pullman car. No bumps or jolts disturbed the passengers' impression that they were gliding on air rather than steel rails. During the first few hours Leslie and his friends were absorbed in observing the exotic grassland outside. And it was a special thrill to spot the fabled River Platte appearing through their left windows—a silver-gray sheet of slow-moving water that glinted like a gunbarrel in the sunshine. Close to the river were strands of willows and cottonwoods. They could trace the river's westward course even when they could not see the water by the trees.

Soon a soft-speaking black porter named Howells brought

out small tables, which he hooked into place at each window. Next Howells carefully laid down a fresh white tablecloth, upon which he placed expensive silverware and goblets of water. It was time for lunch.

The Pullman had its own kitchen at the rear of the car. In it was a coal oven for lamb and beef roasts, a griddle for fried chicken and pancakes, and a charcoal broiler for some of the best steaks on the continent. Meats and vegetables were kept fresh in a large ice chest in the floor. A large wine rack occupied one corner of the kitchen. Fresh water flowed from a pair of large tanks on the car roof.

For lunch the passengers savored delicately chilled fruits and hot cornbread. Then came concoctions of whatever variety the passengers craved—the chef's specialty being broiled chicken on toast with a special herb sauce. And there were potatoes stewed in tomatoes and tossed salads that could have graced tables in any palace. For liquid, one could choose steaming coffee or wine imported from vineyards on the Rhine.

As the Leslie party ate, the train pulled into the town of Fremont, thirty miles west of Omaha. The wheels had not even stopped before men, women, and children from the cheap-fare cars in the front of the train were leaping onto the platform and dashing for the station lunchroom. It was a mob scene, with mothers shoving their children before them, old men elbowing youngsters out of the way, and meek-appearing ladies fighting past them all. The Leslie party, sipping their coffee, felt amused and very superior. When the thirty-minute lunch break was over, the human tide crashed out of the eating room and scurried up the high steps of the passenger cars—many swinging aboard even as the train was beginning to move.

The tugging of the engine to pick up speed, the puffs of

smoke rising from the stack, the *clickety-clack* of the wheels over rail joints, these had become familiar sensations. Yet it was always a thrill to experience them once more.

Upon leaving Fremont, the true power and majesty of the Great Plains descended on them. It was not just the wide expanse of quivering grass. More than that, it was the relationship of the grass with the sky, which now, too, had expanded. The clouds, the prairie wind, and the grass seemed to be part of a universe that they had not been aware of before. In order to have a better view of the impressive scenery on this fine April afternoon, many of the Leslie party moved out onto the rear platform, where some lounged in easy chairs and others stood at the rail to let the wind brush their faces. Their conversation concerned the effect that the quick advance of civilization had on prairie life. Things were changing very rapidly. Remember the buffalo? Only a few years back gigantic herds of a million or more snorting, shaggy-haired beasts would have darkened the landscape around for many miles. The very earth would have trembled to the tattoo of their hooves. But the Union Pacific had carried hunters with rifles into the buffalo's domains. In less than a dozen years the herds had been largely wiped out along the UP tracks. Now the only traces of the beasts were their bones, which lay bleaching along the trails over which they once migrated. "The antelope too are fast following the buffalo," Brace noted. Soon "the principal targets for pistol practice on the train platform will be prairie dogs and ground owls."

Toward midafternoon the train pulled into the settlement of Columbus. Although the town was thriving, it gave the curious impression that it was not permanent, that its wooden stores and homes sticking upright like turkey feathers would soon blow away, leaving not the slightest trace. The town was strictly a creation of the railroad. It lived when the locomotives hooted in and died when they rumbled off.

At Columbus the Leslie party clambered down the steep Pullman steps. The station was packed with local citizens—for the train arrival was the main event of the day. Many persons anxiously tried to sell items to the passengers during the brief stop. Most unusual were the prairie dogs—chubby, squirrel-like animals whose mounded burrows often formed little villages beside the railroad. The hapless creatures were confined in boxes about a foot wide. Those persons foolish enough to purchase them soon learned that they did not survive for long in captivity.

At one end of the station platform some Pawnee scouts leaned against the wind. "The tribe has dwindled to a mere handful," Brace wrote, "since the days, not too far distant, when they lorded it over the Platte Valley, fought the Sioux, massacred the settlers, and dotted with their lodges all the willowy surface of the Plains." Now the men, dressed in worn blue army coats three sizes too large, were warriors without a purpose, no longer able to shoot the vanished buffalo, yet not able to fit into the civilized life that had intruded upon them in the form of the railroad.

As the train continued on its westward voyage, the Pullman passed close to more Indians. At twenty miles an hour both groups had ample time to run their eyes over the other. The Indians saw men and women in elegant clothing relaxing in plush chairs. chatting and chuckling while the great iron horse carried them on a ride so smooth that they could rest their heads against the soft cushions and never experience a jolt. The Leslies saw ill-fed red men on scrawny ponies with dust-spotted squaws tramping grimly behind. "They pass close by the track," Brace Hemying wrote, "and as we rush past them all their faces, hideously shining with red paint, are turned up to our windows and seen for an instant before we leave them far behind."

Two worlds had passed. One forecast the coming Era of

the Machine, and the other portrayed the dying Stone Age.

Not long before reaching Grand Island the Leslies witnessed their first Great Plains sunset. Tremendous masses of clouds heaped up on the horizon in a silent explosion of fleece and froth. The sun caught each rolling mass with rays of gold, leaving the shadowy portions behind blue-gray, like mysterious caverns where Darkness lived. "We have never known before," Brace told his readers, "the height and depth and vastness of the sky . . . the lower world is lost and forgotten in the wonder overhead."

While the passengers watched the brilliant pageant, Howells fastened the little luncheon tables in place. Silently and efficiently, scarcely disturbing their reveries, he brought them cups of soup brewed from fresh oysters preserved in the ice chest beneath the kitchen floor. By the time the passengers had finished this predinner appetizer, the western horizon had turned a lustrous shade of pink, which blended into mauve toward the zenith. Most of the party adjourned to the rear platform. There they sipped frothy drinks while they watched the moon peer over the tracks like a shaven Indian head. They conversed for an hour or so before dinner. And while they amused themselves, the engine carried them another twenty miles onward—the distance a pioneer's prairie schooner would barely have covered after an entire day of dirt, dust, and drudgery.

Dinner was a fabulous repast. Some passengers had steaks, charcoal-broiled to perfection. Others enjoyed roast turkey, with spiced stuffing styled as only the Pullman chef knew how. Dessert was homemade ice cream, an impressive delicacy in the days before refrigeration. The car's interior was lighted by gently swaying lanterns, which gave softly pleasing illumination.

After dinner Frank and Miriam and their guests played cards far into the night, or at least until Howells chided them into letting him make up their beds. These beds were quite comfortable. indeed, the sleeping accommodations were one of the Pullman's most heralded points. Howells first connected each pair of window seats by means of a bench, upon which he placed a mattress, fresh sheets, and blankets. Then he attached voluminous curtains to ceiling fasteners. These he pulled around the bed, thereby converting the space into a cozy sleeping quarter. The lady passengers slept one to a room. But the men had quarters only half as large, for their room also had an upper berth, which Howells pulled down from a recess in the ceiling.

Traveling at night brought special pleasures. Brace, in particular, was fascinated with the experience:

The first night on the plains is probably passed by every curious and enthusiastic traveler in spasmodic efforts to keep awake and see as much as the darkness will reveal to him from his section windows. If there be a moon, the temptation is irresistible; and, drawing back the curtains, he will lie, as we did, dozing, waking, and staring lazily out, conjuring up fantastic shadows in the moonlight of distant teepees, herds of grazing buffalo (which by the prosaic sunshine, would turn out mere barnyard cows,) howling coyotes and dark unknown shapes that traverse the plain with flying leaps and disappear into mystery. Then a warm red star twinkles out near the track, and we come upon some little wayside station, with glowing windows, wide open door, and a wakeful lounger or two on the platform, seen for a second and gone again.

While many of the travelers were half-dozing amid scented sheets, they passed Plum Creek, Nebraska, once a trading post on the Oregon Trail. Sometimes six hundred immigrant wagons a day had lumbered through Plum Creek. Indians, too, had been here, big brazen warriors who often terrorized the migrating families and had actually massacred an entire party of Iowans, save one woman whom they held captive for five months. When the Union Pacific came through, the redmen wrecked a train at Plum Creek. That was past now, however, and the only Indians that Leslie and his companions saw that night were moonlight phantoms.

Sleeping was a pleasureful experience, rocked by the gentle swaying of the cushioned Pullman. But several hours later the train jerked to a sudden stop. The night was black now, and rain splattered violently against the windows. Men and women, in robes. their eyes still squinting with sleep, gathered in the long curtained hall. What could be wrong? they muttered. At last Howells made his appearance, announcing that a freight train had been derailed a few miles ahead of them. It would take a while to clear the tracks to get past.

For a moment the group was silent, knowing the wreck could have been theirs. But the irrepressible party mood was always with them, so while Howells folded up the beds, Leslie and his friends crowded against the windows to enjoy the storm. They had never seen a better deluge. And the wind! It made the telegraph wires shriek. It was so wonderfully wild outside, so grand, so exhilarating that the more adventurous donned their rubber raincoats and descended from the car. As one young lady worked her way through the wind and rain toward a pile of interesting-looking buffalo bones, a gust caught her from an unexpected direction and flung her onto the soggy earth. Her raincoat was whipped to one side, and the rain drenched her instantly. She staggered back to the car, laughing excitedly . . . what fun! Soon the others returned, wet and happy. They had flirted with the primeval elements at no danger or hardship to themselves. When the game was over, they could adjourn to the comfort of the Pullman. That was how life was meant to be enjoyed.

In a few hours there was a gentle tug from the engine, and the train moved forward. Shortly they passed the wreck, caused by half a dozen cows who had decided to saunter onto the tracks at the moment the freight was passing. Later that morning they stopped at Sidney, Nebraska. While the passengers on the crowded coaches made their usual rush to the station café, the Leslie folk strolled leisurely about the little frontier town. Some of the ladies found themselves before a little cabin not far from the bluffs, where they chatted with a black woman. In response to questions, the woman told them: "Over yonder they gambles and fights most all the time, and they kills somebody among themselves every now'n then. . . . There's a lot over there in the buryin' ground that was stabbed or shot or somethin'."

The riotous section of Sidney looked peaceful in the morning sunshine, but the ladies saw in their imaginations the dying gunslingers and knifed dancehall charmers. For a moment their pulses quickened. Then the locomotive whistled them back to the train. Howells brought them drinks, and evil yet alluring Sidney slid out of sight.

The next day the train arrived at Cheyenne, Wyoming, a rollicking town of around 4,000 inhabitants—nine tenths of whom were occupied in the gambling trade. Cheyenne had twenty dens of chance, some of which operated in conjunction with gaudy music halls. Leslie and his friends decided to visit one of these emporiums of pleasure. Pocketing revolvers, they strolled nervously to a long brick building draped with signs which glowed flaming red in the moonlight. They entered through the barroom, overhung by a row of chandeliers glittering with candles. Through the thick cigar smoke they made out a garish painting of Yosemite, with its lean waterfall and majestic bluffs. Edging through the crowd with deliberate "pardon me's," the New Yorkers ascended a narrow flight of stairs to the music hall's second floor boxseats. The box was actually a miniature room with a wide, arched window-opening from which they could see the first floor stage. A pretty young waitress in an off-the-shoulder dress brought them drinks. Noting the large sign saying, "Gents, Be Liberal," Leslie gave the miss a handsome tip.

The show began with the orchestra squeaking out some tunes. Then dancers strutted onto the stage. They were not bad, Leslie had to admit. The highlight of the act came when one girl on a trapeze swung back and forth along the length of the theater. The hall was so narrow that her skirt dusted the box seats and more than one whiskered patron exchanged confidences with her as she floated past. The show went on until two in the morning. Then, tired but pleased with the experience, Leslie and his company strolled toward the Pullman. Cheyenne was still active at this sleepy hour. The crowd was mostly rough sorts such as mountain men in weather-stained buckskin or prospectors with shoulders like those of an ox. They were all courteous however, especially to Miriam and her ladies. But the New Yorkers felt that just beneath the gilded surface lurked violent temperaments that could erupt whenever strong men challenged one another with guns on their hips.

They were glad when they were back in the civilized security of their Pullman. Hardly had they reclined on their soft pillows than the train pulled out. Beyond Cheyenne lay the outriders of the Rocky Mountains. A second locomotive had been hooked onto the first, and the long haul up the mountain front began. Later that day they reached the Dale Creek chasm, over which a magnificent bridge had been constructed—at this time the world's highest. Dale Creek had been long awaited. Brace Hemyng and others rushed to the Pullman platform to enjoy the sensation of crossing on track that seemed as narrow and fragile as a spider's web.

Seen from a distance, this marvel of iron trestle work spanning the deep, rocky bed of the stream has the airiest and most gossamer-like effect; but it is a substantial structure over which our long train goes roaring in safety, though not without a few shrieks from those on the platform who are not used to seeing a hundred and thirty feet of empty space yawning below them.

Some spectators standing with Brace became dizzy and clutched the railing frantically. News of train wrecks was frequent enough to support their concern that a piling or girder might give away, and they would be hurled to the yawning depth. But the heart-thumping bridge was crossed in safety, and the passengers settled down to cards and conversation. Although the route was so steep that the twin engines were puffing vigorously, the grade was smooth, and Leslie's party was hardly aware they were ascending the highest point on the UP. Years ago Colonel Dodge, chief engineer of the UP, had discovered this route when he was chased by Indians. Although the redmen had ruled supreme before the coming of the railroad. now army posts guarded the route, and the way was safe.

Beyond the hamlet of Sherman, atop the pass, lay the Laramie Plains. This was a parched basin long dreaded by pioneers and Indians alike. Most of the land was barren boulders and gravel. Few plants could survive the drought and blistering heat—only low-growing sagebrush the color of dishwater. Yet the Pullman passengers were refreshed by the wind that wafted through ceiling vents, and their drinks always clinked with ice. Thus, whereas in years past, sweating men and women in dirty wagons had seen nothing romantic in the landmark known as Skull Rocks, the Leslie people, cool and refreshed, could marvel at the reddish-gray colors that glistened in the sunshine that seared down from the cobalt sky. The feared Laramie Plains held terrors no longer for persons whisking past on a modern Pullman.

Three thousand inhabitants resided in the town of Laramie, where, before the coming of the railroad, no one at all had lived. The train stopped for dinner there, then was on its way again. As darkness came, Howells moved gracefully about the Pullman with his stepladder lighting the overhead lamps. Follette, Miriam's little dog, yelped at the porter, as he always did. But the good-natured Negro had long since become used to such nuisances and paid the animal no mind. Meanwhile outside it had grown very cold, for it was still April, and the altitude was very high. Snow began to fall, and the passengers enjoyed watching jackrabbits frisk amid the accumulating piles of white. "Lying luxuriously among the pillows of our sofa," Brace wrote, "it is fascinating to stare away into the dimness of the strange, wintry world, to watch the hovering flakes, to follow the scurrying rabbits, and to trace far back in the white mist the weird shapes of solitary buttes."

The Pullman became cold during the night. But the sleepers simply nestled deeper into their cozy blankets. Outside their windows the storm howled, yet they were perfectly comfortable. The train rumbled smoothly on.

As the sun rose on the fourth day out of Omaha, the passengers woke to a snowy world. Sunshine made the snow dazzle like quartz, so everyone dug out smoked eyeglasses. The train thundered over the long Green River bridge and pulled into the station of the same name. Stretching their legs on the platform, the New Yorkers found a cage where a couple of mountain lions were on display. As was the custom, the men tapped their canes against the cage bars and bounced paper wads off the cat's noses. The ladies shrieked properly as the teased animals clawed out at their tormentors. Twenty minutes passed quickly, and the Leslies again boarded the train, leaving the pumas snapping and snarling. During the balance of the morning the train passed through almost endless miles of snowsheds and drift fences—much to the passengers' pouting, for these obstructions blotted out much of the magnificent mountain scenery. One shed engulfed them in smoke and cinders and darkness for more than half a mile.

At Evanston, Wyoming, they came upon their first Chinese, evidence that they were nearing the territory of the Central Pacific Railroad. The Central Pacific had built eastward from California at the same time that the UP had built westward from Omaha—the two lines meeting at Promontory Point, Utah. For laborers, the Central Pacific had relied mainly on coolies signing on from some of China's poverty-stricken districts, just as the UP had relied mainly on Irish shipping out from the dreadfully impoverished Emerald Isle.

Soon the Chinese were everywhere in their blue blouses and trousers. Their hair was always in pigtails, which swung down to their waists. They smiled as the Pullman moved slowly past, their hairless faces and slender silhouettes giving them a child-like appearance that the Leslie group found appealing. Evanston was a UP repair facility, with a large roundhouse and shops and storage areas for the huge snowplows that were so essential in the mountains. The Leslies took advantage of the stopover to visit Evanston's finest hotel. It was tiny, but neat as an ivory carving. Chinese waiters handled the plates as if they were eggshells. Freshly caught mountain trout was the restaurant's specialty. One of Leslie's artists made a quick sketch of a Chinese waiter. Upon seeing it, the man beamed and showed it to his friends. "Heap smart!" he grunted, and the other coolies agreed. The New Yorkers left "covered with glory," as Brace put it.

A few miles out of Evanston, the train entered Utah and started down Echo Canyon. Brigham Young ruled the territory, where the Mormon Church was supreme. "We at once recognize that we are out of the land of the Gentiles and among a peculiar people," was Brace's comment. What struck them most were the houses, painted fresh white, with green shutters, surrounded by neat white fences. They had not seen such pride in ownership since they left Omaha. Also catching their interest were the Zion cooperatives, general stores operated under the patronage of the Mormon Church.

That morning they had picked up a talkative brakeman who sat on the Pullman roof near the brake wheel. When he was not twisting the wheel to slow the car, he chatted with whoever was on the open platform. He told them stories of Echo Canyon—of the days not so long ago when Utah was a separate Mormon principality and the U.S. government dispatched an army to subdue it. The Mormons prepared to fight, and the boulders they had intended to roll down on the American soldiers could still be seen on the bluffs. Fighting was avoided, however, and Utah had taken its place in the American federation.

The train made many stops so the passengers could collect rock souvenirs. The brakeman was especially accommodating to the Leslie women, providing them with some beautiful pale green rocks streaked with garnet. The ladies were thrilled and put the rocks under their seats. Howells knocked against them as he made up their beds and soon the piles were appreciably smaller. "Jes' layin' 'em to one side," the porter said with a smile when questioned. But the rocks never reappeared.

During much of the day the friendly brakeman, leaning down from the Pullman roof, told his female admirers stories about his life on the rails. He was a romantic figure, riding in the open air, his outline cutting the deep blue sky. He had an important position as far as the train's safety was concerned, for the hand-turned brake wheel was vital in controlling their speed on the long down grades.

The main attraction this particular day was the Thousand Mile Tree. The train eased to a stop at the cedar, upon which a sign had been hung at a crazy angle. It was exactly 1,000 miles from Omaha. The Leslies and their friends experienced a regretful moment as they milled around the tree, sipping diamond-clear water from a noisy creek that tumbled nearby. Only two days remained until they reached San Francisco and the glorious trip would be over. They posed for photographs beneath Thousand Mile Tree. Then the engine whistled, and soon they were rumbling westward once again.

Late in the day they reached Ogden. The sun broke against the Wasatch Mountains, bathing the snowy cones in an amber radiance that left them breathless. Ogden was the "clasp on the belt" of the transcontinental line—as Brace put it. For here the Union Pacific and the Central Pacific met. At this point it was customary for all passengers to leave the UP cars and board a waiting CP train. The Leslies were exempted from this tiresome procedure. Instead they spent their time watching the other passengers struggle through the jumble of trunks and suitcases, boxes and bins, where they were yelled at and sometimes rammed into by the baggage expressmen with their wheeled vehicles.

From Ogden the Leslie party took a short excursion aboard their trusty Pullman down a Mormon track to Salt Lake City to visit with no less a personage than Brigham Young himself. They slept that night in their comfortable Pullman on a quiet side track. For the first time in days their car was stationary— and it bothered some of them. They had become used to the swaying of the car in motion and the soft clacking of the track joints. When the train stopped this night, they had trouble sleeping. Something had gone out of their existence. They realized that train life had all but become part of them. They were used to waking with a wild panorama streaming past their pillows. And what was breakfast without the Pullman cook's sizzling bacon and Howells' steaming coffee? Morning meant idling the hours with a sketchbook or in a leisurely game of cards. Afternoon must be spent on the open-air platform watching great white clouds drift over looming mountain tops.

The interview with Brigham Young was not one of the trip's highlights. Miriam Leslie wrote that "we found President Young standing in the middle of his office to receive us, with an expression of weary fortitude upon his face and a perfunctoriness of manner suggesting that parties of Eastern visitors, curiosity seekers, and interviewers might have become a trifle tedious in Salt Lake City." At first the conversation centered on the weather, which bored some of the party. Then pert Miriam launched a rather audacious attack on Young's habit of keeping multiple wives. "What religion can make a woman happy in seeing the husband whom she loves devoted to another wife?" Miriam demanded. A twinkle came to the old man's eyes as he defended the practice. "As a rule, our women are content in trying to make their husbands happy and their homes pleasant," he retorted. Perhaps Miriam, with her sharp tongue and quick wit, would have enjoyed debating that provocative claim with Young, but many of her party were growing restless with the interview. "We at last obeyed the urgent gestures of those who had not been so well entertained as ourself," Miriam admitted, "and rose to depart." Soon their train brought them back to Ogden, and the westward journey was resumed.

The train did not stop at the famous Promontory Point, site of the historic linkup of the UP and CP in 1869. The place had no commercial value and was now almost as desolate as before the railroad had given it momentary fame. The way west was now through one of the most forlorn deserts on the continent. It seemed incredible to the Leslies that right up to a few years earlier pioneer families had forced their way via covered wagon through this inhospitable expanse of sand, rocks, sagebrush and skin-burning alkali. The region was so desolate that Brace imagined even the rocks were decaying. Yet the very bleakness about them served to dramatize how luxuriously comfortable they were in this new era of steam travel.

It was now that they took particular notice of the other travelers who used the railroad for free transportation across the desert. They often saw tramps camped at the railroad stops. As soon as the train squealed to a halt, these penniless hoboes on their way to hoped-for riches in California would dive under the car wheels to coil themselves between the frame and axle. There, half sitting, half lying, they would be carried on as the train moved, dust blowing into their eyes, cinders pelting their legs. The conductors and brakemen were paid to keep tramps off the trains, for they often pilfered passengers' suitcases. But for all the railroad's vigilance, a vagabond or two always managed to catch a ride.

Indians, too, frequented the trains—particularly along the Central Pacific portion, where an agreement with the management permitted them free rides. They loved to stand on the platform between the cars, their faces glittering with scarlet paint as they poked into the wind to gape at the earth thundering past more rapidly than a galloping pinto.

The final lap of the memorable journey began as they ascended the lofty Sierras just out of Reno, Nevada. Night was falling, and it was wet and chilly. Yet Brace and several others wrapped themselves in blankets and braved the windy rear platform, for upcoming was one of the most interesting portions of the trip. As the train, now double-engined again, labored up the mountains, the clouds broke up and the moon danced about the snowy peaks. Beside them the Truckee

River foamed over mossy boulders. It was a beautiful scene.

Carried effortlessly up the rugged mountain face, Brace and his companions recalled stories of the horrendous winter of 1867 that the Central Pacific construction crews spent in Truckee Canyon. From January through April the labor camps were entirely snowbound. Banks of snow were higher than the rooftops, and holes had to be dug up to the surface so the men could receive air to breathe. Work continued on the track-laying in huge snow tunnels. Rocks for the embankment walls were blasted out of the mountains and lowered by ropes and pulleys into the snow tunnels, where they were wedged into position. Avalanches continually hammered through the canyon, sometimes carrying away entire camps. Hundreds of laborers lost their lives, but nobody kept exact count, for they were only Chinese coolies, nameless to their white supervisors.

Now much of the canyon was protected from the snow by wooden sheds that extended for miles—much to Brace's discontent. But at Donner Lake there was a temporary gap in the sheds from which Brace could glimpse the frigid blue-black water of the lake and the menacing mountains that surrounded it. In 1846-47 the Donner party wagoning to California from the east had become snowbound here. By the time spring thaws permitted them to stumble on, half of their party had fallen to starvation and sickness and many had been eaten by their fellows. Brace was greatly affected by Donner Lake, bathed in spectral moonshine. He remembered it as "one of the most vivid pictures of all our journey."

Where the Donners had failed, the steam train had no trouble climbing over the frosty summit, then continuing through a long tunnel at Emigrant Gap. Here, again, the way was so easy that the travelers gave little thought to the sweating coolies who had blasted the tunnel through the living rock, sometimes advancing only eight inches after an entire day's bone-weary labor.

Brace stayed on the platform all night. Sunrise found him describing the vast walls of trees which rose about him like columns of a Gothic cathedral. Then the train came to the head of the American River: one of the most spectacular canyon vista in North America:

> The train swings round on a dizzily narrow grade, with a wall of rock towering above and the almost vertical side of the abyss sweeping down to the narrow bed of the river.... While the train waits and the photographer runs hither and thither with his tripod, we wander along the edge of the track and scramble a few feet down the side of the precipice after wonderful wild flowers. We lie in the fresh, dewy green grass and stare down into the gloomy shadows of the canyon; and the twenty minutes, crowded so full of beauty, seem to be but a second in passing.

They were at the top of a tremendous cleft in the mountains cut by the American River. The canyon walls plunged nearly straight downward for 2500 feet. In the distance mountains rolled away like endless waves of frozen surf.

The train hurried down the valley. There was a half-hour stop at Sacramento, and most of the party took advantage of the time to hire horse carriages and canter down the streets: past homes with flowers in such bunches that the Easterners gasped, past Chinese bazaars jammed with odd curios. Leaving Sacramento, by early afternoon the train had chugged into the Oakland station, built close to the San Francisco ferry dock. The engine hissed for a moment, then died. Brace and the others climbed down and stood beside their Pullman. It was strange to be leaving what had been their home for so many exciting days and nights. Howells was there to say farewell—as was the cook who had provided them with so many sumptuous meals. It had been a splendid journey—one they would always remember. Surely, they agreed, railroad travel was the most comfortable, the most scenic, and the most rapid means of locomotion ever invented by man.

They boarded the Frisco ferry. As it pulled out into the bay, Frank Leslie, Miriam Leslie, Brace Hemying, and the others gazed one last time at the train. It was now suddenly part of their past. For Frank the future held tragedy. When he returned to New York creditors would be howling for payment of the money he owed them. Shortly he would succumb to cancer of the throat and die within three years of his railroad excursion.

Upon Frank's death, Miriam would take over his publishing kingdom. She would succeed where Frank had failed, and at her death four decades later she would leave the bold sum of two million dollars to the women's suffrage movement.

As for the future of Brace Hemying, he of the beautiful word poems of early transcontinental steam travel, we know nothing.

The *Mississippi*, an 1836 steam pot, was much like Peter Cooper's original.   *Courtesy Illinois Central Gulf Railroad*

The "North West Railway Polka" was an attempt to popularize the railroad in 1859. The handwritten note at the top right indicates that the composer gave this copy to her cousin.

Courtesy Chicago and North Western Railway

THE FINEST FARMING LANDS

CORN — COTTON — FRUITS & VEGETABLES
EQUAL TO ANY IN THE WORLD!!!
MAY BE PROCURED
AT FROM $6 TO $12 PER ACRE,
Near Markets, Schools, Railroads, Churches, and all the blessings of Civilization.
1,200,000 Acres in Farms of 40, 80, 120, 160 Acres and upwards, in ILLINOIS, the Garden State of America.

The Illinois Central Railroad Company offer, on LONG CREDIT, the beautiful and fertile PRAIRIE LANDS lying along the whole line of their Railroad, 700 MILES IN LENGTH, upon the most Favorable Terms for enabling Farmers, Manufacturers, Mechanics, and Workingmen, to make for themselves and their families a competency, and a home they can call Their Own.

ILLINOIS

Is about equal in extent to England, with a population of 1,722,666, and a soil capable of supporting 20,000,000. No State in the valley of the Mississippi offers so great an inducement to the settler as the State of Illinois. There is no part of the world where all the conditions of climate and soil so admirably combine to produce those two great staples, CORN and WHEAT.

CLIMATE.

Nowhere can the industrious farmer secure such immediate results from his labor as on these deep, rich, loamy soils, cultivated with so much ease. The climate from the extreme southern part of the State to the Terre Haute, Alton and St. Louis Railroad, a distance of nearly 200 miles, is well adapted to Winter

WHEAT, CORN, COTTON, TOBACCO,

Peaches, Pears, Tomatoes, and every variety of fruit and vegetables are grown in great abundance, from which Chicago and other Northern markets are furnished from four to six weeks earlier than their immediate vicinity.

THE ORDINARY YIELD

of Corn is from 50 to 80 bushels per acre. Cattle, Horses, Mules, Sheep and Hogs are raised here at a small cost, and yield large profits. It is believed that no section of country presents greater inducements for Dairy Farming than the Prairies of Illinois, a branch of farming to which but little attention has been paid, and which must yield sure profitable results.

AGRICULTURAL PRODUCTS.

The Agricultural products of Illinois are greater than those of any other State. The Wheat crop of 1861 was estimated at 35,000,000 bushels, while the Corn crop yields not less than 140,000,000 bushels, besides the crop of Oats, Barley, Rye, Buckwheat, Potatoes, Sweet Potatoes, Pump-

kins, Squashes, Flax, Hemp, Peas, Clover, Cabbage, Beets, Tobacco, Sorghum, Grapes, Peaches, Apples, &c., which go to swell the vast aggregate of production in this fertile region. Over Four Million tons of produce were sent out of Illinois during the past year.

CULTIVATION OF COTTON.

The experiments in Cotton culture are of very great promise. Commencing in latitude 39 deg. 30 min. (see Mattoon on the Branch, and Assumption on the Main Line), the Company owns thousands of acres well adapted to the perfection of this fibre. A settler having a family of young children can turn their youthful labor to a most profitable account in the growth and perfection of this plant.

THE ILLINOIS CENTRAL RAILROAD

Traverses the whole length of the State, from the banks of the Mississippi and Lake Michigan to the Ohio. As its name imports, the Railroad runs through the centre of the State, and on either side of the road along its whole length lie the lands offered for sale.

CITIES, TOWNS, MARKETS, DEPOTS.

There are ninety-eight Depots on the Company's Railway, giving about one every seven miles. Cities, Towns, and Villages are situated at convenient distances throughout the whole route, where every desirable commodity may be found as readily as in the oldest cities of the Union, and where buyers are to be met for all kinds of farm produce.

EDUCATION.

Mechanics and working men will find the free school system encouraged by the State, and endowed with a large revenue for the support of the schools. Children can live in sight of the school, the college, the church, and grow up with the prosperity of the leading State of the Great Western Empire.

For Prices and Terms of Payment,
ADDRESS LAND COMMISSIONER, Ill. Central R. R. Co., Chicago, Ill.

End of track—an early railroad construction scene. The building of the IC opened for development more than 11 million acres of prairie wilderness. As many as 10,000 men were employed at one time in building the 705-mile railroad project of the day.

Courtesy Illinois Central Gulf Railroad

An early Illinois Central poster promotes sales of land near the tracks. Although this copy was hard-sell hype, it did not exaggerate by much the productivity of Illinois' virgin prairie soil.

Courtesy Illinois Central Gulf Railroad

Contrast these two IC locomotives: above, a wood-burning, diamond-stack engine from the 1850's; below, a coal-burner of a type that had become standard by 1865, replacing the less efficient wood-burners.   *Courtesy Illinois Central Gulf Railroad*

OAL-BURNING PASSENGER LOCOMOTIVE.

An IC passenger train puffs into Chicago's Woodlawn station around 1865. Today this bucolic rural scene has vanished under urban build-up and sprawl. *Courtesy Illinois Central Gulf Railroad*

An IC train leaving Chicago in 1864 over the famed Lake Michigan trestle. In later years, the lagoon would be filled in, the tracks covered over, and Grant Park laid out on top.

Courtesy Illinois Central Gulf Railroad

An IC train enters Chicago about 1865. Its right-of-way still follows
the Lake Michigan shoreline, but Madison Avenue (the street facing
the yards and the lake) is today a lineup of skyscrapers and smart
shops.   *Courtesy Illinois Central Gulf Railroad*

A cartoon lures passengers to the line.
                              Courtesy Chicago and North Western Railway

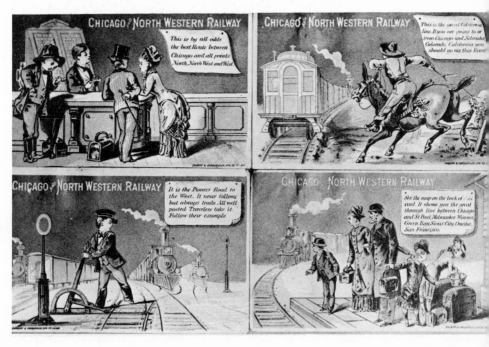

A fascinating one-hundred-year rail saga lies between the small engine of the 1880's dwarfed by the modern diesel.

Courtesy Santa Fe Railway

An old wood-burner pauses for leg-stretching. Notice the cheap-fare passengers packed in the boxcar.

Courtesy Chicago and North Western Railway

An 1879 poster designed to attract train riders West.

Courtesy Chicago and North Western Railway

2,000,000 FARMS of Fertile Prairie Lands to be had Free of Cost

IN

CENTRAL DAKOTA

The United States offers as a Gift Two Million Farms to Two Million Families who will occupy and improve them. These Lands lie between the 44th and 46th degrees of latitude, and between Minnesota and the Missouri River. In this belt is about

30 Millions of Acres

Of the Most Productive Grain Lands in the World. The attached Map shows the Location of these Lands.

THIS MAP SHOWS THE ROUTE of the MINNESOTA AND DAKOTA BRANCHES of the

Chicago & North-Western R'y

AND OF THE

Winona & St. Peter, Chicago & Dakota and Dakota Central Branches,

INTO THE

"FREE" LAND DISTRICT OF CENTRAL DAKOTA.

DISTANCES.

YOU NEED A FARM!

Here is one you can get simply by occupying it. It will be noticed that the

CHICAGO AND NORTH WESTERN

Has Two Lines of Road that run through to these Lands. It is the only Rail Road that reaches them.

In the Districts to the West, North and South of Watertown, are many millions of acres that you can reach by the CHICAGO & NORTH-WESTERN RAILWAY. Along its Line in Dakota have been laid out a number of Towns in which are needed the Merchant, Mechanic and Laborer. CENTRAL DAKOTA is now, for the first time, open to settlement. The Indians have been removed and their reservations offered to those who wish to occupy them.

HOW TO GET THERE

Any Ticket Agent should be able to sell you Tickets via the CHICAGO & NORTH-WESTERN RAILWAY, to TRACY or MARSHALL, Minnesota, or to WATERTOWN, Dakota. At Tracy you can get Tickets to all Stations West on the Line in Dakota. From Watertown, or from any Stations West of Marshall, you can get conveyances that will take you to the Lands West, North or South of the Lake Kampeska Line of the Railroad. All Agents of the CHICAGO & NORTH-WESTERN RAILWAY can sell you Tickets to these Lands.

AT CHICAGO YOU CAN BUY TICKETS AT

62 CLARK STREET; 75 CANAL STREET, Corner of Madison; at the WELLS STREET DEPOT, on Kinzie Street, north of Wells Street Bridge; and at KINZIE STREET DEPOT, on the Corner of Kinzie and Canal Streets.

BEAR IN MIND You can not get to the Lands by Rail Road, unless you go via the

Chicago & North-Western R'y.

Riders enjoy a sumptuous meal aboard a Pullman Hotel Car in this 1878 poster. At night the seats were converted into beds and upper berths were pulled down from the panels above. Curtains gave all the sleepers privacy. *Courtesy Chicago and North Western Railway*

The spectacular head-on crash of the *Lucifer* and the *Lion* locomotives in 1874   *Courtesy Chicago and North Western Railway*

A funeral train waits to take the body of fireman Whittaker to Goldthwaite, Texas, after he and the engineer were killed by a bandit on July 22, 1898.   *Courtesy Santa Fe Railway*

Little Buttercup, built in 1880   *Courtesy Santa Fe Railway*

The first Santa Fe limited chugs toward Los Angeles in 1892. California farmers were absolutely dependent on locomotives like these to haul their produce to Eastern markets.   *Courtesy Santa Fe Railway*

KING DEBS.

Engraving, "King Debs," by W.A. Rogers, from *Harper's Weekly*, July 14, 1894
Courtesy Chicago Historical Society

This 1901 photo shows a locomotive waiting to be rotated onto the proper track after being repaired at the roundhouse.
Courtesy Santa Fe Railway

A long passenger train lets pleasure-loving passengers off before a posh hotel at Redondo Beach, California.   *Courtesy Santa Fe Railway*

An excursion train pauses to permit the well-dressed patrons to pose with four ragged children at the station. This car had oil lights, two double beds, and six single beds.   *Courtesy Santa Fe Railway*

Workmen cut snow into blocks to be hoisted off the railroad tracks during the horrible winter of 1881.

Courtesy Chicago and North Western Railway

A train stops for the passengers to gape at Canyon Diablo. The locomotive is on an old beanpole bridge. A new arch-span bridge has begun to take shape at the left.

Courtesy Santa Fe Railway

Cut-away drawing of an oil-burning Santa Fe locomotive

Courtesy Santa Fe Railway

Another **Powerful** Reason
Why *the* CHIEF
is still CHIEF

The Fastest *and* Most Exclusive train between Chicago and California..

A crack passenger train swirls past a slower-moving freight.

Courtesy Santa Fe Railway

A mechanic tests the air brakes in a locomotive cab.

Courtesy Santa Fe Railway

A freight train ascends a low grade in New Mexico. Cars of trains such as these were often frequented by hoboes.

Courtesy Santa Fe Railway

A Santa Fe passenger train crosses mountains in California. Compare the speed of the train with that of horse-drawn pioneer wagons that once lumbered over trails similar to that in the center of the picture. *Courtesy Santa Fe Railway*

View from the fireman's window in a diesel cab as a steam-driven
freight approaches at full speed.

Courtesy Santa Fe Railway

The crack "400" Limited gathers speed as it rockets out of Chicago
in the 1930's. The super-fast express made the 400-mile run to
Minneapolis–St. Paul in just 400 minutes.

Courtesy Chicago and North Western Railway

A youngster gazes in wonder at one of the last steam locomotives,
preserved as a monument to a vanished age.

7

Titan of the Rails

The crisp autumn air vibrated to church bells. It was 1879, the beginning of railroading's Golden Age. A groom and his bride were escorted from the church by their friends and into a waiting carriage that drove them to a little railroad station in upstate New York. The slouchy young groom did not seem much of a catch for Mary Averell, she who loved music and fine tapestries, and had had a cultured aristocratic upbringing. Even in his wedding finery Edward Henry Harriman was a spindly little fellow with hunched shoulders, a receding chin, and thick spectacles. E.H. probably said little during the carriage ride, for he disdained light chatter. Besides, he was not comfortable in formal dress, preferring his usual baggy suits and weather-worn hats.

The carriage drew up before the station. A locomotive was there, steam hissing from its flanks. On its side, in bright new paint, were letters spelling out "E. H. Harriman." Behind it was a private car for the honeymooners, compliments of Mary's father, president of the line. Although Mr. Averell's railroad ran only through the backwoods portion of the state, a private car was still an impressive way to begin one's married life. Not only that, but Averell had offered E.H. a position on his railroad's board of directors.

As Harriman and his bride settled into their chairs and the train puffed off toward Lake Champlain, E.H. must have thought about this railroad business and the possibilities it offered a young, ambitious person. Yet anyone catching a glimpse of him as the train passed would have chuckled if told that this goggle-eyed little man would, in less than two decades, become one of the most powerful persons in the nation, an individual before whom governors would quake and presidents rant. Through his control of a magnificent railroad empire, he could make or break the prosperity of populous towns. He would bind almost the entire nation into his steel web.

There was little in Harriman's past that indicated his future. He had quit school with a sketchy education at the age of fourteen. Attracted to the Wall Street financial district, he took a job as messenger, for which he received less than a dollar a day. But once on Wall Street, he quickly familiarized himself with the intricacies of financial dealings. His boss was greatly impressed and soon gave him an office job with the informal title of "pad shover." "My capital when I started," Harriman later said, "was a pencil and this"—tapping his head. He saved his thin salary and devoured all the information available about the new industrial age that was emerging in post-Civil War America. It was a jolt-and-jostle time as the wealthy and the mighty carved out economic dukedoms, then lost them to the pirates that prowled the financial shadows.

Harriman's big opportunity came in 1869, the day since known as Black Friday. Two robber barons, Jay Gould and Jim Fisk, had secretly been buying massive quantities of gold. They stood to corner the market and make fabulous fortunes so long as the federal government did not release its own gold supplies. Somewhere along the line, Harriman put his slim savings into the soaring gold market. Then, sensing that the government might be about to release some of its treasure, he sold out just as the price peaked. In this manner the crafty young man accumulated the initial resources that would launch him on his financial career.

At twenty-two Harriman purchased a seat on the prestigious New York Stock Exchange and opened his own brokerage firm. E.H. quickly gained a reputation both for sloppy dress and acute money sense. Soon important businessmen were trudging up the two flights to his dingy office. The largest and most exciting stock trading was done with railroad securities, for these were hot stocks and bonds highly favored by the more aggressive investors. It was easy to make money when railroad profits were soaring and dividends increasing. But Harriman also knew how to make money when times were temporarily slow, by selling short.

Because Harriman was a director on his father-in-law's railroad, he gained insight into how a line was run. Therefore he decided to purchase a line of his own and run it himself. The railroad that he chose as his starter was a little thing that meandered between upper New York and New Jersey. As it stood, it was not worth much. But what interested Harriman was its strategic possibilities. For it could link up with either the giant Pennsylvania system, which could use it to receive coal from the Great Lakes, or with the huge New York Central, which had an important yard at Newark. So Harriman fixed up his line's roadbed and installed a new grain elevator at its terminus. Then he put the railroad up for sale; dangling it between the Penn and the NYC. The Penn finally took Harriman's road, and he made a juicy profit.

Now that he knew how it was done, Harriman raised his sights. He would see what he could accomplish with such big game as the Illinois Central.

The IC was the darling of the financial community. Profits were great as settlers flocked to the prairie to plant the corn that almost burst out of the rich Illinois soil. Harriman had long been convinced that the IC would prove a profitable investment, for he was handling IC stock through his broker- age house for his clients. Thus in 1881, when the assassination of President Garfield sent all securities tumbling, Harriman purchased IC heavily at the low prices. Buy, buy, buy—he felt that the IC was to be the key to his future. Thus, when the smoke cleared in 1883, the obscure stockbroker from New York was one of the IC's largest stockholders.

Harriman now campaigned for a seat on the twelve-man board of directors. In order to become a director he needed the support of someone currently on the board. And Harri- man knew the perfect man to help him. This was Stuyvesant Fish, a tall, blond aristocrat with whom Harriman served as director on his father-in-law's little railroad. Fish was quite different from Harriman. He was used to wealth and loved the spotlight that Harriman shunned. Yet somehow the two oppo- sites got along, and Fish secured his friend a position on the IC board.

Harriman was not the sort of director to be content to grow wealthy sitting in an armchair. Whenever he was in something, he was in it to his eyeballs. Harriman saw the IC not as an impersonal assortment of rails and boiler plates but as a living force which would help mankind span the rivers, girdle the hills, create towns where there were none before. He envi- sioned the IC as an expression of himself as he should have been—a giant among men, with long muscular arms which could roll farm goods down rail lines like bowling balls. Although Harriman might be a puny, nearsighted little runt, his railroad would make him into a titan.

Harriman loved railroads almost more than he loved his wife or his children, more, even, than he loved the income and social position that the increasing IC dividends brought him. And so, allied with Fish, he launched the Illinois Central on an expansion program. Between 1886 and 1888, a line was built across the northern prairies to Freeport, Illinois, and from there a branch went up to Madison, Wisconsin's hitherto isolated capital. Another line reached out to West Lebanon on Indiana's fertile grasslands. Still a third was flung to Cedar Rapids, Iowa, from where yet more lines were spun out to South Dakota's wheat country.

With the Midwest ever more nourished by IC arteries, Harriman turned to new areas. To improve transportation south he ordered construction of a bridge over the formidable Ohio River at Cairo, Illinois. By October, 1889, the wondrous structure was ready for its crucial test. At 7 A.M. on October 29 Harriman (who was now IC's vice-president), Stuyvesant Fish (company president), and a bevy of whiskered notables (including the venerable Roswell Mason) gathered on the approachway to the bridge, which was the longest such span in the world. Indeed, the bridge was such a daring piece of architecture that there was much serious conjecture that it would not stand up to the weight of the locomotives the IC planned to hurl across it. It was in order to disprove such doubts that the ceremonies had been organized.

Around midmorning, nine heavy locomotives grunted up the approachway. These engines were then hooked together. Harriman and Fish climbed into the cab of the lead locomotive. Then, with wild hoots, the weighty iron caravan lumbered up the grading and onto the bridge itself. Harriman had placed his very life on the line in order to convince the public that this long, high bridge was as safe to cross as Grannie's culvert. The crowd on the banks was tense as the nine 75-ton Mogul locomotives inched along. Their wheels made the rails squeal, while far below the Ohio River snapped angrily against the pylons. Steamboats backed well away, for the fear of collapse was on everyone's mind.

Harriman watched the bridge girders tremble as the locomotives grunted past. In his youth he had loved excitement. He was an accurate rifleman and a passable boxer. But these were the adventures of youth. Railroading had become his passion as an adult. Here was adventure that neither the hunt nor the ring could match. The fireman brushed close to Harriman, his muscles rippling as he heaved more coal into the firebox. Harriman could see the flames dancing like angry devils. He felt the drive wheels surge with steam power. Meanwhile the girders moved past, and the wild river churned impotently at his feet. Then someone in the cab gave a shout as the Kentucky embankment was reached. The bridge had withstood a far greater weight than it would ever be exposed to under normal conditions.

Let other men seek their particular avenues of pleasure. To E. H. Harriman the joy of railroading surpassed anything on God's planet.

Big as the IC was, Harriman began to seek new challenges. The financial panic of 1893 provided him with just such an opportunity. The mighty Union Pacific had bought too many branch lines and could not meet a government loan as it fell due. None other than J. P. Morgan, the most powerful banker in the nation, tried to reorganize the company, but could not. The Jacob Schiff banking group took over, but found its efforts hampered by a mysterious force. After investigation, it was discovered that the opposition was headed by "that little fellow Harriman," as one banker put it. Small in stature though he might be, Harriman had suddenly emerged as a giant in the railroading world. Schiff, second only to Morgan, confronted Harriman and demanded what price he would take to stop his harassment. Harriman coolly announced that there was no price. "I am determined to get possession of the road," he grunted.

When Schiff smiled as he thought of Harriman's puny personal finances as compared with Schiff's great assets, Harriman reminded him that he was the guiding force on the giant Illinois Central. Because the IC was the best-run railroad in the nation, its credit was so strong that it could borrow at a rate lower even than that Schiff could obtain. Harriman said he would gain control of the UP by merely issuing $10 million in IC bonds. With that Schiff sobered. He not only put Harriman on the UP board of directors, but acknowledged that if he proved himself a strong leader, he would end up with the chairmanship.

Harriman proceded to dominate the other directors, most of whom were strong men in their own right. Harriman's eyes blazed when he talked. His voice sounded like steel on steel. His ideas were hurricanes tearing away the cobwebs that were suffocating the railroad. He would not be bound by what others whimpered about the UP. There *was* a way to make America's first transcontinental profitable, and, damn them all, he would find it! With this in mind Harriman set off on a personal inspection trip in 1898.

Never before, or possibly since, has a railroad been examined so minutely by one of its directors. Harriman requisitioned a special train—one with the engine in the rear and his personal observation car in front. Several UP officials were with him, as were two of his daughters. He positioned himself on the observation platform, notebook in hand, to scrutinize every mile of track over which the train slowly moved. When it became too dark to see, he ordered the engineer to pull to a siding, where Harriman would spend the night in the luxury that only a Pullman Palace Car could provide. Next morning, when the sun was still tangerine, he would set off once more.

This trip was a satisfying experience for Harriman. He loved the power that his position with the railroad gave him. The trip enabled him to see this power in its most visible form. Gangs working on the roadbed nodded respectfully as his train passed. Employees in every station showed him the greatest deference. Everywhere his slightest utterances were obeyed, for west of Omaha the UP kept the ranchers, cattle-men, wheat farmers, and town merchants alive. State govern-ments might change, and no one would care much. But let the UP flounder, and not all the rifles of the West could save the region from ruination. Harriman was to be their savior. It was a dazzling role to play. And Harriman loved it.

He constantly asked penetrating questions. Like the time when the train stopped for water, and he queried the division superintendant: "Why does it take so long to fill the locomo-tive?" The official answered that the feed pipe only permitted a certain water flow. Harriman then wanted to know why a larger pipe was not used.

"It can't be done, sir," the employee replied firmly. "The engine couldn't take any larger pipe."

Harriman surveyed the locomotive. It was true. Most men would have let the matter lie there. But Harriman was not most men. Delays for water cost the railroad money, for a train at rest was not bringing in revenue. "Then we'll get bigger engines," was Harriman's blunt reply. And so he did.

The Union Pacific became Harriman's baby. He got to know it intimately—from the magnificent depot at Omaha to the small blistered stations in Wyoming. Though many persons derisively called the UP "a streak of rust on a lot of ties," Harriman was convinced he could turn it once more into a premier line. When he returned east, he demanded that the board give him authority to spend $25 million on immediate improvements. After this was done, he invested $300,000 of his own money in UP stock—a sum which would spiral into a vast fortune in the coming years. He spent the directors' money with what some thought irresponsible abandon. "Wasteful and extravagant," was one comment. Others held their breath. "It was a courageous outlay," one banker gasped. But for Harriman nothing was too good for the steel creature he had befriended.

Harriman got his larger locomotives, a whole fleet of them. And he purchased freight cars with more carrying capacity. Then he ripped up most of the track and replaced it with heavier rails. He also replaced the wooden ties with sturdier ones. And, in many areas, he reballasted the roadbed. He literally remade the line in his own tough, lean image. Indeed, so great was the force of his personality that within a single year he was elected chairman of the board.

It was soon apparent that Harriman's program was paying off in added revenue. But a basic problem remained. The UP was a road "from nowhere to nowhere," as its critics claimed. Beginning at Omaha, far from the populated East, and ending in the alkali deserts near Salt Lake City, the UP ran through land of great potential yet meager present resources. In order to ensure the line's future Harriman had to have a good outlet to the West Coast. This was supposed to be furnished by the Central Pacific. But the CP was as rundown as the UP had been. If Harriman owned the CP, he could tend to that. The problem was that the CP was controlled by the Southern Pacific, a really huge line which, running from New Orleans all the way to San Francisco, far outdistanced the Union Pacific. Not only was one-third of the United States tributary to the Southern Pacific, but its steamer fleet linked the United States with Shanghai on the China coast. The SP was, in short, the greatest transportation system in the world.

Collis Huntington, who ran the Southern Pacific, was not a man to trifle with. He had dominated the Big Four who built the Central Pacific. Through his immense wealth and power he was the unquestioned ruler of California and the surrounding states. When a friend once told him he could not take his money with him after he died, Huntington snapped, "Then I won't die." But there are powers even stronger than Huntington, and the old man did die in 1900. The clods were hardly heaped on his grave when Harriman pounced on the Southern Pacific.

It was impossible for Harriman to gain control of the SP using his own finances—no man in the world was that wealthy. The key to Harriman's takeover was the UP, where revenues had doubled in just two years. The result was that the UP was now in a position to borrow large sums of money with low interest. So Harriman simply floated a $100 million UP loan and used the proceeds to buy enough SP stock to gain voting control of the monster railroad. When the SP was his, Harriman boasted to an associate, "We have bought not only a railroad but an empire."

The Harriman System, as it was being called, now dominated wide swaths of territory from the Missouri River to Oregon and from the Gulf of Mexico to the Pacific Ocean. It was an area comparable to that claimed by the Caesars or Napoleon. But in distinction to them Harriman had won his holdings without firing a shot or losing a man. His goal was to build, not destroy. His cavalry was horses of iron, not sinew. And when Harriman had passed through the land, he left it bountiful, not scorched. The whole system hinged on economics, not military force.

It took huge revenues to keep the locomotives running, to maintain the roadbed, to repair the bridges, to pay wages to the army of trainmen and dividends to the host of stockholders. In order to attract the passengers and shippers who would pay the revenues, Harriman was determined to keep his railroad in top condition. This meant all his new holdings, too. First he directed his attention to improving the Central Pacific, since the UP depended on this line to service its Pacific clients.

Once again, as with the UP, Harriman did not spare the hard cash. The CP wound like a coiled snake as it ascended the grades across Nevada. To straighten the line would cost millions, but it would speed up service and enable one locomotive to do the work of two. Thus it would be cheaper in the long run. So Harriman gave the go-ahead, and soon his construction crews were swarming over the parched desert blasting through hills, rather than winding around them, spanning rivers at the shortest point rather than allowing the track to drift along the banks until a cheap crossing was found. Two miles of new tunnels were bored, and eight million pounds of steel was forged into new bridges. When the dynamiting was over and new tracks were laid, 450 miles of Huntington meanders had been replaced by 200 miles of Harriman main line.

Even more impressive—perhaps the master engineering achievement of Harriman's career—was his trestle across the Great Salt Lake. The idea was not Harriman's, but when it was presented to him, he endorsed the bold concept. Few others would have had the daring, the tenacity, and the financial assets to undertake such a feat. Harriman assembled a navy in the Great Salt Lake, and work was begun. The lake bottom was mud and quicksand, and in places was thirty feet deep. Yet the pylons were sunk and the trestle slowly extended across the open water. When the work was completed, it was the talk of America.

While Harriman was reconstructing the CP, he also turned his bespectacled gaze on the Southern Pacific. He flattened an entire hill to improve the SP entry into San Francisco. He regraded the railroad at Burbank and saved seven miles of curving track. He bought half a thousand heavier locomotives and spent $9 million on steamships. Everywhere along the route he threw up new bridges and laid heavier track. All together he spent well over a billion dollars in today's currency. Yet the SP revenue swelled tremendously and more than covered the debt he had created. Both the SP and the CP became prosperous lines in the Harriman System.

It had been relatively easy so far: buy control of a poorly managed railroad, spend a lot of other peoples' money to fix it up, make the road profitable, then garner a personal fortune as his stock increased. But in 1905 Harriman met a worthy adversary. This was God Himself.

An Act of God, as mankind so quaintly puts it, occurred in the California desert when the Colorado River broke through an ill-conceived dam and began flooding into the rich Imperial Valley. The California Development Company could not control the dashing water and asked Harriman for help, since Southern Pacific rails served the irrigated area. Harriman told the company officials that he must receive 51 percent of their stock before he would bring the SP into the fray. When this was done and Harriman was in control of the Development Company, he rolled up his sleeves. It was now E.H. against God. It was to prove an exciting contest.

Harriman put Epes Randolph in charge of the problem. He gave Randolph $200,000 and waited for results. During July and August Randolph built a new, stronger dam, and for a while it seemed that this would do the trick. But one day a flood swelled the Colorado and washed Randolph's fancy dam and Harriman's money off to Mexico. Yet Harriman was not dismayed. He had not gotten where he was by tight-fisting greenbacks—especially when they were borrowed. He wired Randolph $750,000 more and told him henceforth to tend to the Acts of God in the Imperial Valley. Randolph worked with a frenzy. The Colorado battled him almost as if it had a will of its own. River waters whiplashed around the valley, forcing the SP to re-lay up to sixty miles of track—not once but five times. Randolph ordered in three hundred UP side-dump cars and ten trainloads of rock, and built a separate branch railway to accommodate the influx of trains and material. Using a steam-boat on the river, he worked the rocks into earthworks to seal the river into its bed. But in a single day of wet fury the Colorado broke down this earthwork as if it were a palisade of sand built by a child.

It was now that Harriman began to wonder if the battle didn't call for reinforcements from the federal government. Most of the valley belonged to Washington anyway. Besides, it would only cost Harriman $40,000 to rip up the SP tracks and rid himself of the whole problem. And so he wired this infor-mation to President Theodore Roosevelt. But the brassy Rough Rider had no affection for the crafty little financier who had never swung a cavalryman's saber or charged an enemy on San Juan or any other hill. Roosevelt had called Harriman an "undesirable citizen" and was even then unleash-ing the Interstate Commerce Commission on him. Thus Roosevelt wired Harriman back that the government would take the matter into consideration and notify Harriman of its decision sometime in the future. Harriman knew that TR was telling him that the SP could jolly well drown in the Colorado for all he cared.

Now Harriman realized he had an alligator by the snout. He could not walk away from the flood, not with the Interstate Commerce Commission investigating him. Yet he wasn't sure he could tame the mighty river, which was gushing into the Imperial Valley in a stream a half mile wide. Day by day the new channel was becoming more entrenched. Harriman must act with vigor or the river would flood away his financial resources entirely, at the same time that it was washing away the Imperial farmland. "I gave directions to suspend all other work," Harriman later told a friend, "and to give this job the right-of-way over everything else, regardless of disturbance of traffic or of expense. . . . I used every ounce of driving power I possessed to hustle the job as I have never hustled any job before."

Harriman had accepted a responsibility that even the President of the United States shirked. Yet somehow it exhilarated him. Damn the cost; that no longer mattered. This was now combat between titans. The break would be closed simply because E. H. Harriman willed it. He marshaled all the resources of his railroad system. An army of men was mustered from all over the Southwest. More than a thousand pilings were driven into the break. Then six thousand carloads of rocks were tumbled against the pilings. The angry river was severed into a hundred channels that hissed like wounded rattlesnakes. One by one each of these channels was squeezed out. Finally, after the expenditure of many millions, the Colorado was locked into its old riverbed.

Harriman had won. To the end of his life he regarded this as his greatest single achievement.

Despite challenges by the elements, Harriman still hungered for new conquests. In particular there was a tantalizing railroad plum dangling just within his reach. This was the Chicago, Burlington & Quincy. Through it Harriman's Union Pacific could not only gain access to the railroad crossroads of Chicago, but could tap the cotton-hauling roads which linked up at St. Louis. Just as he readied his forces to move on Burlington stock, he was shocked to learn that the railroad had been gobbled up by James J. Hill, possibly the only man in American business who would dare take on E.H. Allied with Hill was the mighty House of Morgan, the most powerful banking concern in the nation.

There were at this time five major transcontinental railroads. The Santa Fe was independent, but Harriman controlled the Southern Pacific and the Union Pacific. Hill dominated the Northern Pacific and the Great Northern. Hill was supreme in his territories. Not only did his lines provide the only outlet for the farmers' produce in the northern Great Plains and the Pacific Northwest, but many of the landholders owed personal allegiance to Hill, since he had transported them from Europe to America for the insignificant fee of $10, the only stipulation being that they settle along one of Hill's lines. Hill needed the Burlington's access to Chicago just as much as Harriman did. But this did not make Hill's annexation of the Burlington any more agreeable to E.H., who was not accustomed to being thwarted in any enterprise to which he committed himself.

The two men were like sovereigns of independent nations. Just as in international politics, Hill's action brought warfare—more subtle than the clash of military battalions, but warfare nonetheless.

Harriman planned his counterattack with the skill of a five-star general. A direct assault on the Burlington was clearly impossible, with Hill's men now deeply entrenched. But there were other ways to march against an enemy. So Harriman moved. James J. Hill was on a leisurely inspection trip of his realm and didn't realize that Harriman's troops had slipped through his outer defenses until he noted a strange upward rise in the price of Northern Pacific stock. Somebody was obviously making large purchases, but who? Because he did not own an outright majority of NP stock (only enough to outvote anyone else), Hill felt that he must hurry to New York, financial center of America, to find out what was happening. Hill, in Seattle, had his private car hitched to a special train, ordered the rails cleared, and sped toward New York. As Hill's express roared across the nation, other trains pulled off the main track to let him through. For this was the supreme ruler of the North. Hill's whims were other men's commands.

Once in New York, the burly Hill banged into the offices of banker Jacob Schiff, who headed Harriman's eastern legions. Schiff admitted he had been buying into the NP; indeed, he boasted that Harriman probably had control of the railroad by this time. And, with the NP in Harriman's hands, the Burlington, its subsidiary, would also fall to him. Hill stormed out of Schiff's office and hustled over to the House of Morgan. Morgan's lieutenants wired their banker chief, who was vacationing in Europe, for permission to lash back at the attackers. Morgan gave his approval, and the main battle began.

The two armies met on the floor of the New York Stock Exchange. It happened that both sides needed just a few thousand shares to have an NP majority. As they began bidding for the remaining shares, the price of NP stock rose from $114 to $150. Then it shot up to $200 per share. Both Harriman and Hill plunged ahead, trampling the small traders who had sold short, hoping to buy the stock when it had dropped. The casualties grew as the stock zoomed above $750. As last it peaked near $1,000!

At this point both Harriman and Hill paused, stunned by the financial ruin which lay around them. The public cried out against the giants who had little concern for the general welfare as they played war games with their railroads. Harriman had been the aggressor, and it was on him that the outcry centered. He was portrayed as a merciless manipulator, glacial cold, obsessed with his ambitions, caring not a jot for those who were maimed as a result of his reckless assaults.

Both Harriman and Hill were forced to admit they had battled to an impass. And so a compromise was reached. Harriman received a seat on the Burlington board of directors and a Union Pacific representative was allowed a Northern Pacific directorship. Furthermore, the Burlington was forbidden to extend its lines westward in competition with the UP.

But Hill kept control of the lines, and some said that he had got the best of Harriman. It was not so, for when Harriman began unloading his northern railroad stock shortly thereafter, he came out with a colossal fortune of fifty million dollars. Although he had not been able to snatch the pair of transcontinentals, the foray had gained him the additional financial muscle that he needed for an even more ambitious scheme. This was an around-the-world transportation line.

With this goal in mind, Harriman had bought the Pacific Mail Steamship Company, thereby obtaining access to rich seaports from Tokyo to Canton and Singapore. He wished eventually to extend his transportation system through Manchuria on the South Manchurian Railroad, then across Asia on the Trans-Siberian Railroad, ending at Leningrad, where Harriman ships could take people and goods to European ports or across the Atlantic to the United States. Harriman felt that the Russian Czar would be glad to lease him trackage on the Trans-Siberian, for it earned very little revenue on its run through the frosty wastelands. The real problem would be the South Manchurian line, which the Japanese had just acquired as a result of their victory in the Russo-Japanese War. In order to induce the Japanese to allow him trackage, Harriman set out for Japan in August, 1905. With him were his wife, his three daughters and two sons, and the vice-president of the Pacific Mail Steamship Company.

They vacationed briefly in Honolulu, stopped at Midway Island, than made landfall at Yokohama. Word had preceded them that this prince of American business was on his way. Most Japanese leaders were avid to have Harriman's investments, since they were badly in need of capital as a result of the Russian war, and the South Manchurian Railroad was in wretched disrepair. A dose of the Harriman regimen was just what it needed. Accordingly Harriman was treated royally. His hotel became the center of the Japanese social world. He was invited to luncheons, garden parties, and banquets, often escorted by the Prime Minister himself. Everywhere Harriman was called upon to speak about the wonders of his railroad ventures.

"From New York to the Pacific Coast," Harriman told the Japanese, "and from there to Japan, about ten thousand miles, the railroad and steamship lines are practically under one control and one management. The economies of operations, the comfort to the traveling public, and the advantages to shippers of this concentrated control can be readily appreciated." It took little imagination to see what could be gained by a transportation system that extended around the world. With a single management team taking care of the routing, the cargo handling, and the financial arrangements, the benefits of using the Harriman System would be tremendous.

Harriman was even granted an interview by the Japanese emperor, a rare honor bestowed only upon the most important foreigners.

From Japan Harriman went to Peking, where the Chinese kowtowed as if he were a potentate, not just a mustached little American. Korea was the third leg of the triumphant procession, which took him over 3000 miles in the Far East. When he returned to Japan, the Prime Minister was there to greet him. Japanese government representatives helped conduct meetings, which seemed to agree to allow him his use of the South Manchurian Railroad. He set sail for home on October 12, 1905.

As Harriman stood on his ship cutting across the Pacific, he must have been elated. The world was parting for him just the way the ocean waves parted before his ship. With each new acquisition more money flowed into his treasury—money that could be used to purchase ever more railroads, steamship lines, and the economic facilities that would enable him to bind the world into a gigantic Harriman network. It is impossible to know where Harriman's boundless ambition would ultimately have led him. Railroads had unlocked the riches of the world to one of the few men with the finances, the experience, the burning vision, and the aggressive instincts to take advantage of the unique situation. Perhaps Harriman could have established a new world order. His lines might have webbed every industrial country, uniting them in a community of transportation where each nation specialized in producing the goods for which it was best suited. Their economics might have become so intertwined that none would have had the resources to have warred upon another. So, too, might his railroad board have become a sort of Congress of the Nations, with the most responsible people of each country sitting together.

But the moment passed. The Japanese, fearful of Harriman's enormous power, broke off negotiations, and not even the silken Jacob Schiff, who visited Japan in 1906, could bring the Japanese back into Harriman's camp. Yet, even without the Japanese, Harriman moved ahead. He expanded his American system by securing a directorship on the Erie Railroad, which now ran from the Hudson River to Chicago.

In 1909 Harriman was sixty years old, certainly not overly aged in a nation where Supreme Court justices often functioned quite well into their upper seventies. It had been just eleven years since he gained control of the Union Pacific. Now he dominated, in addition to the UP and his original Illinois Central holdings, the Central Pacific and the Southern Pacific, and had powerful interests in the Erie, the Baltimore and Ohio (remember Peter Cooper?), the Santa Fe, the Chicago and Northwestern (which gave his UP entry into Chicago), the Central of Georgia, and several lesser lines. His shipping company extended his holdings to the Orient.

Harriman was everywhere active in his economic empire. Although presidents of his individual companies tended to the everyday operation of their units, Harriman supervised the plans for expansion, for modernization, for new financing, for hiring and firing important executives, for coordination of each line with his transportation system. Yet he still had time to plan for new acquisitions. Thus, when a government investigator asked E.H. how long he would continue accumulating properties, he answered without hesitation, "I will go on as long as I live."

In many ways Harriman was lucky. He had entered the business world at the precise moment when the railroads had created an opportunity for power that had never existed before. He had seen what could be done and he had the strength of will and the daring to do it. But he was forced to operate out of a frail human body. And this body could not keep pace with the self-consuming intensity of his brain. By 1909 Harriman's physical endurance was giving out. His stomach could not hold food. The pain which had bothered him for the past two years intensified. He went to the baths in Europe, but they did no good. At last he retired to his mansion in the Ramapo Mountains, near the Erie Railroad, which he may have loved more than any other line. There he sat on his porch, keeping track of the stock market while he waited for the end. Dreams of what might have been hovered like dust motes around him. Another decade of life, that was all he would have needed. J. P. Morgan visited him and the two talked for several hours. Ah, what they could have accomplished had they ever joined forces!

Meanwhile the sands in Harriman's hourglass sifted low . . . and ran out. . . .

8

The Dragon Empire

Chicago was the linchpin of an empire of steam and steel that completely engulfed the country at the end of the nineteenth century. Here lines from the industrial East and the cotton-producing South met those from the corn and wheat regions of the Midwest and the Great Plains. All Chicagoans were aware of the rails that arrowed through their city in all directions. On the lakefront was the smoky Illinois Central yards. Not far to the west were the terminals of the New York Central, one of the giants of American railroading, and the good old Erie, struggling as ever to avoid the junkyard. Nearby were other great termini, where freight and passengers swung into the city from lines originating in distant San Francisco. The Santa Fe ended in Chicago, too, as did the Burlington, James J. Hill's booty which linked the vast Pacific Northwest with Chicago via the Great Northern and Northern Pacific.

The Chicago depots were always jammed with travelers from all over the nation—all over the world, in fact. Everyone took the train to get where he wished to go. There were bejeweled grandees from New York's Park Avenue and the perfumed byways of Paris, businessmen from Boston, Philadelphia, or the dark steel region around Pittsburgh, politicians campaigning for local or national offices, and, of course, the humble persons fresh from the farm or the immigrant ships, who crowded out from the cheap cars toward the front of the trains—talking quietly to conceal their unease in the strange environment dominated by the bellowing mad dragons.

Beyond the depots were the railroad yards. Here acres of tracks were beaded with innumerable freight cars bearing names that sounded like poetry: the Monon of Indiana, the Denver and Rio Grande, the Seaboard Coast Line of Florida, the Canadian Pacific, the Soo Line from Upper Michigan, the Cotton Belt with its blue lightning insignia. Near the yards were squat warehouses and tall elevators fat with corn, wheat, and other grains brought in from the city's vast trading domain. There were always wagons groaning between the freight yards and the storage buildings. The sound of cursing teamsters mingled with the rumble of their wagons, the whinnying of their horses, and the screech of the train wheels. Behind it all was the constant *chug-chug-chug* of the stocky little switch engines that scurried about the yards like mechanical caterpillars.

Above the freight yards and depots and warehouses was a gray pall of smoke. It enveloped everything with a layer of grime and a sooty odor. The smoke slithered down all Chicago streets, and even filtered through cracks in closed windows, leaving a telltale layer of dust on mantles, glass panes, and tabletops.

Railroad activity permeated almost every aspect of Chicago —as it did, to a lesser extent, nearly every major American city at the turn of the century. The railroads seemed to exist by and for themselves—seemed to run on their own volition, not on the will of the creatures who claimed to own them. Even the men in the board rooms sometimes doubted that they had much real control over the monsters whose movement made the earth shake and upon whose existence the commerce of the entire nation had grown to depend. Under the spell of the locomotives, railroad directors, who were ordinarily humane individuals, turned sharp and cold and worked with near demoniacal intensity to meet the demands of the locomotives. One of these was Mr. George Pullman of Chicago.

George was not a bad sort of chap. Born into a family of ten children, he learned to advance himself by dint of hard work, persistence, and planning for the future. Because he loved to tinker with his hands, he began his career as a cabinetmaker. But railroads fascinated him, and when he migrated to Chicago a few years before the Civil War, he determined to use his woodworking expertise to make a sleeping car which would not rattle out a person's teeth on an overnight run. Accordingly, he fashioned his sleeper as a luxurious vehicle, spending $20,000 on each car rather than the $5,000 which the ordinary sleeper cost. He also made his cars a full foot wider and two and a half feet higher than the others. Although he was warned that railroads could not use these large cars without altering bridges and station platforms, Pullman was insistent. He began production of his Palace Cars, and they were such an immense success that he soon had to build a larger manufacturing plant.

As plans for this new plant developed, Pullman decided he would go further. He would include around it an entire community for his workers. The homes here would be far superior to those a laboring man and his family might be able to obtain in nearby Chicago, where rent-hungry landlords squeezed every penny out of their tenants. The homes in the town that modest George named after himself were neat, well-built structures of eye-pleasing yellow brick. Most of them had five rooms, including a bathroom with a real toilet—something not too often found in Chicago's dreary tenements. The Pullman Company kept the homes in good repair and even provided free trash collection.

In Pullman's town one-tenth of the area was graced by green parks, one of which contained a miniature lake for boating and swimming. Trees shaded the streets, which were not of dirt or cobblestones but of clean macadam. There were free schools, at which the children of the immigrants, who comprised three fourths of the 20,000 inhabitants, could learn English and the American customs which would enable them to better themselves. Pullman provided a theater for performers and musicians, and a library, of which the initial 5,000 volumes were a personal gift from George himself. During the summer the eighty-piece Pullman Military Band gave concerts—and one year was even good enough to earn the state championship.

However, Pullman did not erect his town entirely from a spirit of goodwill. He viewed his model town as an economic, rather than a philanthropic, enterprise. Thus he designed the rents to be sufficient to cover all expenses plus a profit of 6 percent. Pullman had a perfect right to expect profits from his homes—and 6 percent was not unreasonable in good times. The problem was that when the depression of 1894 fell upon the land, Pullman kept his rents high while, at the same time, he lowered the wages he paid his workers. When his workers complained about the wages, Pullman remained firm, stating that he must decrease his expenses if he was to meet the competition of other sleeper manufacturers. As for the rents, they were an entirely separate matter unrelated to wages. It was not his function to provide subsidized housing for his men and their families. Good business principles dictated that he keep rents as high as the workers would pay without moving to other areas.

With low wages and high rents, the workers were truly in a bind. There were instances where a man spent an entire week laboring in the plant, then, after his rent and the food he bought at the company store were deducted, he received less than a dollar. Things grew even worse when Pullman began laying off some of his workers, because the depression had lessened demand for his Palace Cars. Men, women, and children were now almost destitute. Their clothes were in tatters, they had almost nothing to eat, they could buy virtually no fuel for the cold nights to come. Yet they feared to leave Pullman's town to go to areas where the rents were 25 percent lower because then the company would probably not hire them back when times got better. Still, they could not earn a living at Pullman. What could they do?

In desperation they sent a delegation of forty-three workers to discuss their grievances with George Pullman. The Big Man insisted that he could lower wages as he saw fit—it was not their place to tell him how to run *his* company. As for the rents, that too was his business; the city belonged to him—every brick, every windowpane, every blade of grass. And just to let the workers know who was in charge, Pullman fired three men from the committee the very next day—thereby violating a pledge his representatives had made to the men. The workers felt the company was trampling them to death. They had no alternative but to call a strike. Their goal was to force Pullman to raise their wages to a subsistence level. On May 11, 1894, the strike began.

The workers knew their only chance of success was to secure the support of the American Railway Union, a vigorous, growing organization which had taken the measure of James J. Hill when it prevented him from lowering wages. Although the union was only around a year old, it was headed by Eugene

Debs, a dynamic genius who had marshaled more than 150,000 trainmen under the ARU banner. It happened that the ARU was holding its first national convention in Chicago that June. A Pullman delegation appeared at the convention and made an impassioned plea for union support. "We struck at Pullman because we were without hope," a Pullman worker cried out to the delegates. "We joined the American Railway Union because it gave us a glimmer of hope. Twenty thousand souls—men, women, and little ones—have their eyes turned toward this convention today, straining eagerly through dark despondency for a glimmer of the heaven-sent message you alone can give us on this earth." He called their strike a "dance of skeletons bathed in human tears," as he pictured the frightful conditions in Pullman, where the company management refused to meet with them, waiting confidently to see them broken and humiliated. Now their last hope was that the American Railway Union would go into the battle as their champion.

Eugene Debs was not eager to become involved. Although the ARU had won a minor tilt with Jim Hill, the underpopulated northern plains could not be compared with steel-spun Chicago, the central bastion of the railroad empire. Debs knew that once the ARU entered the fray, it would turn from a simple affair of a few thousand workers against a single employer to a full-fledged war which would pit the working class against the steamy brawn of the railroad industry. This industry was the most titanic business confederation that had ever existed. Yet Debs and his lieutenants could not resist the soul-wrenching appeal delivered by the strikers.

Debs tried to bargain with Pullman. Six ARU members along with six strikers went to the company, but no official would even speak to them. A second attempt at a conference was likewise met with by a company stonewall. At last the ARU sent Pullman an ultimatum: either he would open some sort of negotiations within four days or the ARU would order its members to boycott Palace Cars. When Pullman remained adamant, Debs reluctantly decreed that no ARU member would switch any Palace Car onto a train. If the railroad line fired the switchman, all ARU members on that line would cease work. The boycott began at noon on June 26.

As Debs had foreseen, the Pullman strike now took on a greatly magnified aspect as the railroad warlords accepted the challenge with pleasure—for they saw it as an opportunity to snuff out the ARU. The directors of the twenty-four lines running out of Chicago formed the General Managers Association. They had combined assets of nearly a billion dollars. They declared that no upstart union should force them to operate their trains without the Palace Cars, which they rented from Pullman. Accordingly some ARU switchmen were fired, and the strike was on in Chicago. Soon the ARU boycott spread to twenty-seven states and territories. A Chicago newspaper called it "the greatest battle between labor and capital that has ever been waged in the United States."

When the general managers recruited toughs from eastern cities as strikebreakers, Debs could see that the stage was being set for violence, which would be an excuse for the railroads to call for state and federal soldiers to ensure the movement of the trains for the public good. Thus Debs frantically wired all his leaders to insist that their men use no strongarm tactics to prevent the movement of the trains—especially the United States mail cars. Yet it was impossible for Debs to restrain everyone, particularly in Chicago, which was then filled with hundreds of drifters and troublemakers left over from the Columbian Exposition. "No more dangerous place for such a strike could be chosen," the U.S. Strike Commission later testified. And the superintendent of the Chicago Police said that even with more than 3,000 men on constant duty he could not ensure the peaceful movement of the trains, for "this city is practically a network of railroads . . . [it is] filled with tracks, yards, towers, switch houses, and freight houses."

Lawless elements beyond union control spiked switches, wrenched out rails, detached freight cars, and blockaded the tracks with overturned cars. As the transportation began to break down, it became apparent to the public just how important railroads were to their way of life. Nearly every item of commerce moved by rail. There simply was no other efficient means of transportation, only the outmoded horse-drawn wagon, and even this was useless for long hauls since all the interstate roads had been allowed to deteriorate until virtually the only byways which now remained were those that ran to the railroad depots.

It was in the railroads' interest to instill panic in the public and their elected officials. The newspapers had no time for truly investigative reporting. When reporters saw incidents of violence, they assumed that they were being carried out by the ARU—an impression encouraged by railroad press releases. The newspapers tended to emphasize the spectacular; which made exciting reading and sold newspapers. Thus headlines proclaimed "Mob Is in Control" and "Law Is Trampled On." The archenemy to law and order was "Dictator Debs."

The climax came with an incident on July 2, 1894. By means of hyped-up reporting, the newspapers and a pro-railroad United States marshal on the scene misrepresented a group of 500 onlookers as a crazed mob of 3,000 ruffians. A single frieght car that had been derailed through an error on the part of the assistant yardmaster became a number of cars smashed up and wedged against the tracks to prevent the passage of United States mail trains. Good-natured gibing by the crowd gathered to see the mishap became jeers and hoots. The words of a dozen winos were transformed into a mob cry: "To hell with the Government!" "To hell with the President!"

Although it could not be established that any of the active crowd members were under orders from the ARU, Debs and his union were blamed for the incident. The federal marshal informed Attorney General Richard Olney that "I am unable to disperse the mob, clear the tracks, or arrest the men who were engaged in the acts named, and believe that no force less than the regular troops of the United States can procure the passage of the mail trains." Olney, a staunch railroad supporter, carried the report to President Grover Cleveland. Olney pointed out that two federal judges had already issued an injunction prohibiting Debs and the other ARU leaders from engaging in any deed which might encourage the boycott of the Pullman Palace Cars. With this legal backing President Cleveland ordered the entire command of Fort Sheridan to be dispatched to Chicago.

The troops arrived on July 4, Independence Day. On the next day violence reached its peak. Dozens of railroad cars were thrown across the tracks and burned. The damage ran to nearly a half million dollars. Chicago was in chaos. Debs urged his ARU strikers to leave the vicinity. Apparently almost all followed his advice, for not a single ARU man was killed or wounded in the excitement that ensued. Nevertheless Debs was blamed for the "unparalleled scenes of riot, terror and pillage," as the newspaper headlines put it. On July 10, Debs and three lieutenants were indicted by a federal grand jury in Chicago for conspiracy to obstruct a mail train. Debs eventually went to jail for six months.

The strike was broken. Pullman reopened his plant, filling a quarter of the positions with new personnel. The remaining workers had to sign a pledge to join no union. A thousand of the old employees were left almost penniless, saved from actual starvation by last-minute relief contributions from the general public.

The railroads had won a complete and utterly smashing victory. At the end of the century their power over America could not be challenged.

The Pullman episode had not only tied up Chicago, but had reached as far as California, where a young writer named Frank Norris had observed the futility of the workers' actions with a compassion born from his boyhood in Chicago. Norris had spent his first fourteen years there in a fashionable home on Michigan Avenue near the Illinois Central yards. After studying creative writing at Harvard, upon graduation he had obtained work with a West Coast magazine. But article writing did not satisfy his yearning to create something big. Eventually the realization came to him that nothing could be bigger than a novel about the railroads.

Norris had a deep respect, even a kind of reverence, for the railroads. Yet, because the railroads were so all-powerful, he also seriously mistrusted them. This mistrust was not based on the Pullman strike alone. The monumental abuses of the railroads were a continuing public scandal. The railroads were constantly devising schemes to maximize profits. The most obvious way was simply to charge very high shipping rates. This became particularly bad at points along the line where there was no competition among the various lines. Indeed, a Minnesota congressman had reported to the House of Representatives that railroads in his state were making far more profits from shipping wheat than the farmers did from growing it.

The incident which solidified Norris' decision to write an epic railroad novel occurred in an area of California controlled by the Southern Pacific. The SP had encouraged settlers to occupy railroad-owned lands, with the understanding that the land would eventually be sold to them at a moderate price. After the farmers had improved the land and its value had accordingly risen, the Southern Pacific had offered it to the farmers at prices as much as eight times what they had expected to pay. The farmers had revolted and refused to leave their farms even after the SP sold the land to new settlers. The SP thereupon called in the local law enforcement, and when the farmers resisted, five of them were killed and many more arrested.

Norris saw in the incident the plot for the epic he hoped to write. It was the people against the railroad, which was reaching out with long, octopuslike tentacles to squeeze out the independent entrepreneurs and bring all the others under its domain. *The Octopus*, as Norris named his story, became one of the most ambitious American novels up to that time. It helped end the era of romantic stories and open that of realism. It was, in short, a landmark in American literature.

One of the central figures in *The Octopus* is a poetically inclined young writer named Presley. Like Norris himself, Presley was around thirty years old and had a degree in literature from an eastern college. He was highly sensitive to the wrongs of the world. Staying at the home of the most influential of the valley ranchers, Magnus Derrick, Presley soon found himself enmeshed in the ranchers' fight with the Southern Pacific, which Norris renamed the Pacific and Southwestern. The year was around 1900, just before E. H. Harriman took over. Thus Norris' railroad president is not the wily little Harriman, but a massive old man with an iron-gray beard—probably a takeoff on the feisty tycoon Collis Huntington.

Presley's first personal encounter with the railroad was one night as he made his way home after a visit to an enchanting Spanish mission. He had to leap for his life as the locomotive hissed past, making the earth quiver and "filling the air with the reek of hot oil, vomiting smoke and sparks; its enormous eye, Cyclopean, red, throwing a flare far in advance, shooting by in a sudden crash of confused thunder; filling the night with the terrific clamour of its iron hoofs." And when it had snarled off, Presley found the mangled bodies of sheep which had not escaped the merciless monster. All was "a hideous ruin in the engine's path."

To Presley the locomotive stood for all that was satanic in the world. He hated even its whistle call, which he remembered as "ominous notes, hoarse, bellowing, ringing with the accents of menace and defiance." And he saw the locomotive as "the symbol of a vast power, huge, terrible, flinging the echo of its thunder over all the reaches of the valley, leaving blood and destruction in its path." It was "the leviathan, with tentacles of steel clutching into the soil—the soulless Force, the iron-hearted Power, the monster, the Colossus—the Octopus."

Presley's friends, the ranchers, were the righteous opponents of the evil railroad, whose rates they wished to lower. Magnus Derrick farmed ten thousand acres—a vastness of wheat that tossed golden bright almost as far as the rim of the world, or so it seemed to Presley. When plowing time came, the ranchers provided work for hundreds of extra men. They used huge plows, each drawn by ten steaming horses, to turn over the soil that would mother the wheat to nourish the world. Sometimes a line of plows stretched out for a quarter mile. To feed the workers a row of tables as long as a bowling alley was set up. Chinese cooks prepared the food—large chunks of beef and hot breads, finished off with ample drafts of wine. The ranch owners often ate with their men. But they were not one with them; they were far above them, so Norris has us believe. They were tough feudal lords, bowing before no one as they turned the wilderness into fields of bounty. They were worthy to take on the malicious railroad, which lusted for profits only, caring not a coal clinker for the sacred land. Thus Norris presented a strongly prejudiced view of the railroads. But it was a view that found many supporters throughout America. And it was a view that had a great many truths—as well as half truths—to support it.

The railroad rates were passed on by the state railroad commission, an elected three-man council. The commission had traditionally been in the P&S's pocket, its agent having bought out each of the commissioners. The P&S had also bribed judges, so that the ranchers stood little chance of winning rate decreases in court. They could not even go to the state legislature, for the railroad's million dollar lobby at Sacramento kept key lawmakers in line. The railroad controlled the governor, too—and here fiction merged with fact, for one of the Big Four who built the Central Pacific, Leland Stanford, had actually been California governor for a few years.

Formidable as the railroad was, the ranchers were defiant. A hundred of them vowed to take on the octopus. With Magnus Derrick at their head, they moved to the attack. Magnus was confident. But his wife was not:

> Annie Derrick feared the railroad. At night, when everything else was still, the distant roar of passing trains echoed . . . straight into her heart. At such moments she saw very plainly the galloping terror of steam and steel . . . symbol of a vast power, huge and terrible; to oppose which meant to be ground to instant destruction.

The ranchers formed a group called the League. Heading the League was a small committee run by Derrick. Although the League members at large believed Derrick would pursue honorable means to combat the railroad, he had reluctantly put aside his scruples. His first objective was to get his son, Lyman, elected to the Railroad Commission. To this purpose he contacted the corrupt Democratic bosses in San Francisco. Together they made a few well-placed bribes, and Lyman was nominated at the state convention. Then they joined forces with a small railroad that was a rival of the mighty P&S and thereby brought this railroad-controlled commissioner to their side. Lyman campaigned on the promise of cutting the railroad rates by 10 percent, and when he was elected, he began examining the P&S rate schedule.

On the surface the ranchers appeared to have won. Yet the railroad fought back. One rancher named Dyke felt the counterattack first. He had long been uneasy, for he knew the railroad had a reputation of devouring opposition. Dyke seemed to feel "under his feet . . . below him in the dark the huge tentacles silently twisting and advancing, spreading out in every direction, sapping the strength of all opposition, quiet, gradual, biding the time to reach up and out and grip [him] with a sudden unleasing of gigantic strength."

Dyke was about to commence a bumper harvest. Therefore he walked into the shipping office to arrange for freight cars to haul his bonanza. The rate was two cents a pound, but Dyke expected to induce the railroad to lower it to a cent and a half because of his volume. However, the P&S clerk eyed him and calmly said that the rate was now five cents and there would be no bargaining.

Dyke was staggered. It would be impossible for him to pay such an exorbitant rate. When he protested, he was told he could ship some other way. But there was no other means to get his produce to the eastern markets. He was caught—and he was ruined. Yesterday he had a fortune growing in his fields and today he was a pauper. "What's your basis of applying freight rates, anyhow?" he cried out.

"All—the traffic—will bear," he was told, slowly and deliberately. Norris was not writing fiction here. Where a railroad was without competition, it often was likely to charge the very highest rates it thought could be squeezed out of its shippers.

But what of the ranchers' Railroad Commission? When Magnus Derrick asked his son, Lyman, when he was going to lower the rates, Lyman answered evasively that it was not as simple as it seemed. "The man who, even after twenty years' training in the operation of railroads, can draw an equitable, smoothly working schedule for freight rates between shipping point and common point, is capable of governing the United States. . . . Cut rates; yes, any fool can do that; any fool can write one dollar instead of two, but if you cut too low by a fraction of one per cent and if the Railroad can get out an injunction, tie you up and show that your new rate prevents the road from being operated at a profit, how are you any better off?"

Again Norris spoke the truth, for the problem of railroad rates was extremely complicated. In actual testimony before the United States Senate a few years earlier, a railroad executive defended the charging of higher rates in areas where the railroad had no competition on grounds that these were regions of thin population where the railroad would otherwise not earn enough to maintain its trackage and shipping facilities. In many cases this was correct, and the railroad could prove it was justified in charging differential rates.

However, the ranchers in Norris' story did not agree with such a philosophy. They did not intend going broke to demonstrate that the rates were unjustifiably high. Under pressure from Derrick, Lyman finally came up with a plan to reduce the rates by 10 percent, thus fulfilling his campaign promise. But it was a sleight-of-hand schedule that slashed the rates in certain deserted areas by more than the required amount—yet left rates much the same in the wheat-producing region. Magnus Derrick and the other ranchers were furious, for it was obvious that the railroad had gotten to Lyman. Lyman protested that the P&S had paid him nothing, that fair play had dictated his decision. Yet when Lyman later ran for governor, it was noted that the railroad helped him win the election. This was hardly startling to Norris' readers, for many an election had a lingering odor of train smoke around it.

With the commission out of their control, Magnus Derrick and the League prepared for the onslaught they knew was coming by organizing a private army of six hundred farmhands and cowboys. However, the League's weak point was not in guns but in the fact that its members did not actually own much of the land that they ranched, having leased the railroad's alternate sections with the understanding they could eventually purchase them at around $2.50 an acre. Now the railroad declared that the value of the land was $27 per acre and that this land was being put up for sale to anyone who agreed to purchase at that price.

When the notification of this intention was read at a gathering of the ranchers

A dozen men were on their feet in an instant, their teeth set, their fists clenched, their faces purple with rage. . . . The sense of wrongs, the injustices, the oppression, extortion, and pillage of twenty years suddenly culminated and found voice in a raucous howl of execration. For a second there was nothing articulate in that cry of savage exasperation, nothing even intelligent. It was the human animal hounded to its corner, exploited, harried to its last stand, at bay, ferocious, terrible, turning at last with bared teeth and upraised claws to meet the death grapple.

Norris could hardly have been more graphic in his hatred for the railroad, although bared teeth and upraised claws may have been a bit strong.

The League fought back in court as it tried to prove that the railroad had obligated itself to accept the lower rates for their land. But when the court ruled against the League, the fight became desperate. The railroad put the ranchers' leased land up for sale. Many buyers suddenly appeared, happy to pay $27 per acre—particularly since the railroad itself was financing them. When the sales were completed, the P&S began surprise evictions. A United States marshal and a dozen armed deputies descended on the home of one rancher and flung his possessions into the road. Next they headed for the home of Derrick himself. When the ranchers learned the news, they had no time to gather their army. Instead Derrick and ten others leaped on their horses and galloped to a place where they could head off the lawmen. There they waited with loaded guns, and, we presume, teeth bared. This was much as the farmers had done in the incident upon which Norris based his novel.

When the posse members were sighted, Derrick and two others lay down their weapons and met them in the open, trying to dissuade the marshal from taking possession of their land. The other ranchers, looking on from a distance, could see the deputies apparently begin to encircle the three ranchers. Then a deputy's horse, startled when it scraped against a wagon wheel, knocked down one of Derrick's companions. With that a watching rancher who mistakenly thought the deputy had intentionally abused his friend, dropped to one knee, whipped his rifle to his shoulder, and fired. The posse returned the fire, and the fight was on. Several volleys roared before either side realized what was happening. Then the shooting quickly stopped. But several deputies and five ranchers were dead.

The shock of the incident ended the League's resistance. The railroad's buyers took over the land. Derrick, deprived of his ranch and his reputation, became a broken old man. The might of the steam empire had again carried the field.

The Octopus struck a chord in American consciousness that gave the novel wide appeal. Everyone felt the vast power of the iron beasts, which had been created by man but which man himself seemed incapable of controlling. The railroad was not subject to the laws of man, only to the laws of nature, that demanded it grow and multiply. Presley, the story's poetic observer, found this out when he confronted the great Mr. Shelgrim, president of the P&S. Shelgrim refused to become excited about the killings. "You are dealing with Forces, young man, when you speak of Wheat and the Railroads, not with men. . . . Men have only little to do in the whole business. If you want to fasten the blame of the affair on any one person, you will make a mistake. Blame conditions, not men."

Presley was confused. "But you are the head of the Road," he stammered.

Shelgrim shrugged his massive, rounded shoulders. "I can NOT control it. It is a force born out of certain conditions, and I—no man—can stop it or control it." The locomotive was a god unto itself, "huge, terrible, a leviathan with a heart of steel, knowing no compunction, no forgiveness, no tolerance; crushing out the human atom standing in its way with nirvanic calm, the agony of destruction sending never a jar, never the faintest tremor through all that prodigious mechanism of wheels and cogs."

Steam engines were the dispensers of evil as well as good to the turn-of-the-century American. The depth of America's love for these mechanical wonders could only be matched by its fear of their power.

9

The Wild Drama
of Adventure

S tarlight gleamed on the rails as the big Overland Express sped southward from Sacramento, California. Suddenly the engineer caught a flickering far down the line. Soon he made out a flagman signaling him to stop. The engineer yanked on the brakes, and the locomotive slowly ground to a halt.

As soon as the engine was no longer moving, two men emerged from the bushes and ran to the foot of the cab. Over their heads they had masks made of old underwear legs with ill-cut holes for the eyes and mouth. At first the engineer thought they were playing some sort of joke on him. But he noticed the cartridge bandoliers around their chests and the Winchester rifles pointed at him. This was no game; it was a damned stickup. Sam Browning and Jack Brady, the outlaws, forced the engineer and his fireman to climb down from the cab and to walk to the Wells Fargo express car, which was carrying gold and silver to the East. With a rifle barrel poking into his back, the engineer begged the messenger in charge of the shipment to open the car door. When the Wells Fargo man said he wouldn't, one of the robbers yelled back that they had a couple sticks of dynamite and could just as easily blow the door apart. Their argument was compelling, and seconds later the boxcar panel slid to one side.

Browning and Brady leaped into the car, the engineer and fireman ahead of them. Ah, there was the money, stashed in a corner. Fifty thousand dollars—enough to buy them half a lifetime in Mamie's pleasure palace! The engineer carried the four bags of coins to the locomotive. Then the crooks ordered him to pull the pin linking the engine and the coal car with the rest of the train. Once this was done, one outlaw opened the throttle, and the locomotive chugged off, leaving the empty Wells Fargo car and the rest of the Southern Pacific's crack Overland sitting impotently astride the tracks.

It had been handled most shrewdly, the two agreed as they streaked along in the night. It would take the train crew hours to reach a station from which the telegraph could spread word of the robbery. By that time they would have the treasure well buried. After the hubbub died down, they'd dig up the booty and spend it. Soon they halted the locomotive in a deserted area, removed the money bags, and sent the engine racing backward down the track, thereby not only disguising where they had disembarked but discouraging anyone who might be pumping after them on a handcar. Possibly they remembered tales of the Andrews' raiders a generation earlier. As the unmanned locomotive rumbled obediently on down the track, the two pushed through the brush to a likely burial spot. With much grunting and clanging of shovels they dug an ample hole and stuffed the bags into it. Then they refilled the hole and sauntered off. The perfect crime.

The night was quiet after the pair left. Stars swung slowly across the sky. Then a bush parted, and a wide-eyed little tramp surveyed the scene. He couldn't believe it. He had been sleeping nearby, had been awakened by the digging, and had watched the bandits bury the four heavy money bags. It was a dream come true. When he was sure the two were gone, he feverishly uncovered the money, removed ten thousand dollars for his current amusement, and reburied the rest in a place where those who might covet his possessions would not rediscover them.

When Browning and Brady returned several days later, they were flabbergasted to find only a grinning hole where their treasure had once lain. After their yells of rage had died, they reconsidered the matter and decided that train robbery was a pretty quick way to accumulate a fortune. So a few months later they boarded the SP's Number Three at Sacramento. When the train was well out in the country, the two climbed up the side of the baggage car, crawled precariously over the coal car, and reached the engine. Leveling pistols at the engineer, they commanded him to stop the locomotive. But the Southern Pacific trainmen were prepared to deal with crooks by now, so, as the engineer slowed the train, he fixed the brakes so they would not release the wheels until they were reset. He also stopped the train gently so there was no slack between the cars. This would make it impossible for the bandits to draw the coupling pin and escape with the locomotive.

Browning and Brady were unable to fathom the engineer's trickery as they strained over the coupling pin. While they were trying to dislodge it, the engineer scampered off into the brush. Now they were left with a trainful of grumbling passengers and a locomotive that they could not move. Perhaps robbing trains was not what it was cracked up to be. The two stomped off, cussing.

Ernie King recalled this and many other train anecdotes as he wrote his memoirs of a lifetime on the Southern Pacific. He remembered the notorious Dalton Gang, who picked off good old Number 17 at Alila, California, in 1891. And there was Big Burt Alvord, who hauled $80,000 from an SP train near Cochise, Arizona. Big Burt was captured and spent some time in jail. When he was released, he vanished. No one ever knew where he went, but rumor had it that he gathered in the swag, which he had hidden, and spent the rest of his days a most happy gringo in some foreign country.

Most colorful of the SP bandit escapades was that incident of 1895 when two cowboys stopped a train near Willcox, Arizona, and dynamited the safe. In the explosion eight sacks of Mexican silver dollars were scattered about the countryside, making it impossible for the cowboys to find them, but delighting the horde of hunters who spent the next few months scouring the sands. Busiest of the desperadoes were Evans and Sontag. They hit a train each year from 1889 to 1892, obtaining something like $8,000—and leaving five dead men. As with nearly every robber, the pair was ultimately tracked down by their ostentatious spending habits. Sontag was killed, and Evans was escorted to the Big House.

Even our earlier acquaintances, Browning and Brady, came to untimely ends. On their last train robbery, as they marched down the aisles plucking gold watches and other goodies from the nervous passengers, they didn't know that Sheriff John Bogard was on the train. When Browning stalked into the rear car, Bogard was waiting for him behind one of the seats. The sheriff's revolver spat, and Browning fell with a bullet neatly lodged in his heart. Brady, however, surprised the sheriff from the rear and plugged him in the back. Then, leaving the loot, Brady leaped from the train and ran to a nearby bridge, under which he and his deceased partner had previously hidden getaway bicycles. He peddled off into the dust, but was later captured at Sacramento and served nineteen dreary years pounding rocks.

Ernie King recounted only the robberies on the SP. But

there were heists on all the lines—for the railroads were just too tempting. Some of the bandits were colorful and became local heroes. Others were true blackguards, the most vicious of villains. A train robber's fame seldom outlasted the steam era. But tales of one will probably survive as long as legends of American railroading endure. This man was the notorious Jesse James.

Jesse was a tall, rangy sort of person, with dark, almost silken hair. He was extraordinarily handsome. His sense of humor was always with him, even during his most daring forays. Jesse loved children, was gallant with the ladies, and neither drank nor smoked. His father was a Baptist minister, who taught Jesse to shun profanity and carry the Bible. Jesse was basically a God-fearing, clean-living person. He had only one major personality quirk—he loved to rob trains.

Jesse, and brother Frank, four years his elder, grew up in Missouri along the rough Kansas border. During the "Bloody Kansas" era just before the Civil War, the James brothers' sympathies were with the Southerners, for their roots were in the South. When the war began, Frank James rode with William Quantrill, leader of the most feared band of guerrillas ever to scourge the American heartland. Frank was with Quantrill when he led 450 ruffians against Lawrence, Kansas, in 1863. The guerrillas had a marvelous time. The town was nearly demolished, and 182 mostly unarmed persons were killed.

In retaliation Union militiamen, hardly better than ruffians themselves, harassed those families whose relatives were believed to be Quantrill men. The James farm was among those visited, and Jesse's stepfather, Reuben Samuel, had a noose thrown around his neck. When he refused to give information as to Quantrill's whereabouts, the rope was tossed over a tree limb, and he was yanked up and down four times. Jesse, a lad of fifteen, watched with horror from a cornfield. Then the militia spotted him. Jesse was captured, and his back was lashed bloody. Jesse, vowing vengeance, joined the Quantrill group and participated in a fury of skirmishes, murders, and ambushes until the war ended.

After the war Frank and Jesse attempted briefly to live a normal life. But many of their pro-South friends were gone, and the new neighbors regarded them with hostility for their activities with Quantrill (who finally got a justly deserved fatal bullet in Kentucky). When Jesse was expelled from the Kearney Baptist Church, he turned to crime—possibly without too much regret.

Between 1866 and 1868 there were a rash of bank robberies. Some of the outlaws were identified as former Quantrill bushwhackers, and it is probable that Frank and Jesse were among them. By the early 1870's it was more than probable. The James boys were pistol-packing all right. Stories of their daring began to titillate the public. For example, there was the escapade at Kansas City. Despite a crowd of 10,000 jamming the fairgrounds, three horsemen approached the cashier. One dismounted and muttered in a low voice, "What if I was to say I was Jesse James, and told you to hand out that tin box of money—what would you say?"

The cashier retorted in a surly voice, "I'd say I'd see you in hell first."

"Well, that's just who I am—Jesse James," the stranger grinned menacingly, drawing a revolver. "Now you better hand it out pretty damned quick or—"

In some accounts there was a bit of gunplay, and a little girl in the crowd was wounded. But whatever happened, the three desperadoes obtained the cash box with $1,000 and then thundered off, while the bystanders and the shaky cashier gasped in amazement. Such was the audacity of the act that many persons could not help but express admiration for it. John

Edwards of the *Kansas City Times* even wrote a front-page editorial lauding the outlaws:

There are men in Jackson, Cass, and Clay counties—a few are left—who learned to dare.... With them booty is but the second thought; the wild drama of the adventure first.... What they did we condemn. But the way they did it we cannot help admiring.... It was as though three bandits had come to us with the halo of medieval chivalry upon their garments and have shown us how the things were done in the days that poets sing of.

Poets had not sung of train robberies, but the James boys turned their attention to them nonetheless. The whole experience was new at that time—some even claiming (incorrectly) that Jesse invented the whole enterprise. Jesse's first fling came in 1873 when he and Frank and five cohorts dressed in Ku Klux Klan masks wrenched out a rail near Council Bluffs, Iowa, just as a Rock Island train was rounding the bend. The engineer saw what they were doing and hit the reverse lever. The train began sliding to a halt, but the momentum carried the big engine through the gap. It tore into the earth and fell heavily onto its side, crushing the engineer to death. With Jesse directing, the bandits took $2,000 from the express-car safe, then marched through the passenger cars, jabbing their revolvers toward the riders, demanding money, watches, jewelry, and other valuables. Once they had their loot, they mounted their horses and rode into the woods, waving their hats and shouting wisecracks.

When news of the holdup and the engineer's death became known, a posse formed. By careful questioning, the pursuers were able to trace Jesse's route as he headed back toward Missouri. The posse also received accurate descriptions of Jesse's physical appearance. But the problem was that there were no photos available from which Wanted posters could be drawn. And when the Missouri newspapers printed accounts of the train robbery, Jesse himself wrote a letter to the St. Louis *Dispatch* denying the whole affair. This letter was conveniently posted from the distant Montana Territory, to which Jesse said he had fled to escape an unfair trial, which would have resulted had he allowed himself to be taken into custody.

Jesse did not stay in Montana very long, as the public learned when a train robbery took place at Gads Hill, a hundred miles south of St. Louis. Late in the afternoon of January 31, 1874, five men marched into the depot and took control at gunpoint. Then they placed a flag beside the track, which was the standard way of halting trains. As the train puffed to a stop, the bandits boarded her. First they got the big stuff, an estimated $22,000 from the express safe. Then they leisurely tramped down the aisles, guns drawn, pausing before each passenger. The ladies were not robbed nor was any Southern person. Neither were males whose hands had working calluses. Thus began the legend that Jesse was a modern Robin Hood, taking only from the rich, honoring women, and loyal to his beloved Confederacy. Although Jesse seems to have forgotten the rules imposed by this legend more than he remembered them, the aura of medieval knighthood was to linger about his name and his deeds.

Whatever the fantasy about Jesse, it does appear that he had a sense of humor. As the bandits were leaving the train at Gads Hill, Jesse handed a crewman a paper upon which he had written out his own account of the incident for the newspapers—leaving a blank space where the amount of the loot could be inserted. The usual posse was formed the next morning, but the bandits made good their escape.

As a matter of fact it was getting rather difficult to form posses once the men learned that the James gang was the object of the search. For by now it was realized that Jesse and Frank James, with their great shooting skill and rather wild dispositions, would make things more than hot for any posse that had the misfortune to catch up with them. Few farmhands cared for that kind of sport. And actually some Missourians were rather proud of their home-grown highwayman, who, newspaper editor John Edwards wrote, "has more prowess, more qualities that attract admiration and win respect" than the more effete robbers that the East produced. It was Missouri, Edwards continued, "which breeds strong, hardy men—men who risk much . . . men who go riding over the land, taking all chances that come in the way, spending lavishly tomorrow that which is won today at the muzzle of a revolver." In the James boys Southern manhood had risen once again.

Not everyone in Missouri was enthusiastic about the exploits of their native son. The state had many citizens who had fought against the South. And even among the Southerners a considerable portion resented the state's association with lawlessness and gunplay. Governor Silas Woodson was among that majority which felt the state was being gravely injured by its reputation for banditry. With persons like the Jameses running around, immigration and business development would suffer. For this reason Woodson offered a $2,000 reward for "the arrest and delivery of the bodies of said Frank and Jesse James." The railroads likewise put out rewards. But more than that, they contacted the powerful Pinkerton National Detective Agency. In this particular period, the Pinkertons were not the people to fool with. They would often use any tactic—legal or not—to apprehend the person or persons they'd been hired to catch.

After the robbery at Gads Hill Pinkerton men began appearing in Missouri. The first was Johnny Whicher, a twenty-six-year-old daredevil. Whicher's plan, as he told it to the bank president and former sheriff of Liberty, Missouri, was to go to the farm of Jesse's mother, Mrs. Samuel. He would secure employment there and capture the James brothers when they visited. It would be very simple—or so he thought. Accordingly Whicher hopped the freight for Kearney, arrived there about dusk, and began walking to the James farm, which was four miles away. But Jesse's secret network must have gotten word to him, for Jesse and three buddies intercepted the Pinkerton man. The next day his body was found outside Independence.

Now the Pinkertons intensified their manhunt. Two detectives, Louis Luff and Johnny Boyle, went after the four Younger boys, members of Jesse's gang. Abetted by former deputy sheriff, Eddie Daniel, they began snooping around the area frequented by the Youngers. At one home they asked directions of an old man while John and Jim Younger were actually eating lunch out of sight. After the Pinkertons left, the Youngers armed themselves and rode after them. Surprising them, they ordered the three lawmen at gunpoint to remove their weapons. Boyle then spurred his horse and escaped, but both Lull and Daniel dropped their gunbelts. Then while the Youngers debated whether to kill them, Lull flicked out a small pistol he had concealed in a pocket and banged a bullet into John Younger's neck. As Lull galloped for freedom, John caught him in the back with a full shotgun load, while Jim Younger dispatched Daniel. Both John Younger and Lull died of their wounds. The Pinkertons had lost two employees and had only turned the remaining Youngers—Jim, Bob, and Cole—into more deadly adversaries.

When the vicious gunfight made the newspapers, Governor Woodson felt even greater concern for Missouri's soiled reputation—as well as for his own chance of reelection. Eastern journalists were calling Missouri the Bandit State, and way off in Europe presses were recounting the Gads Hill episode as symptomatic of the American West. As for Jesse, he gloried in the notoriety. He even dared to come up from the underground for a public wedding in April, 1874—marrying his cousin, Zee Mimms. The ceremony was attended by fifty friends and was conducted near the bride's home in Kearney, Missouri. Jesse gave a lengthy interview to a reporter while supposedly waiting for a boat to take him to Vera Cruz for his honeymoon. The news item eventually gave birth to a flurry of stories about Jesse's adventures in Mexico, although Vera Cruz was probably just a ruse to lead the Pinkertons on a foreign chase while Jesse remained comfortably in Texas.

Eventually, wife or not, Jesse felt the urge to go back to his life's occupation, robbery. On December 7, 1874, the Jameses and Youngers relieved a bank in Mississippi of $5,000. A day later the gang was at Muncie, Kansas, holding up a train. The James gang had extraordinarily good luck on this heist, carrying off $30,000 in their saddlebags. In these exploits they had their supporters at large. Many cheered them as Southerners getting even with Northern businessmen. Others claimed they were only doing in a spectacular way what many a railroad director did when he quietly palmed off worthless bonds on the unsuspecting public. Nonetheless the rewards increased, and the Pinkertons continued to swarm the countryside. Late on a January night they struck.

Believing that one or both of the James boys were secretly visiting their mother, the Pinkertons surrounded the farmhouse. When the lights were out and the family asleep, the detectives poured oil over a large mass of cotton, lighted it, and tossed the flaming mass into the kitchen. Awakened by the smoke, Mrs. Samuel and her husband grabbed pokers and shoved the fiercely burning cotton into the fireplace. Then a detective hurled a second fireball through the window. As the Samuels flailed at it, the mass suddenly exploded, sending iron shrapnel everywhere. One piece struck Archie Samuel, nine-year-old half-brother of Jesse, in the side, killing him within an hour. Another struck a black servant. A third mangled Mrs. Samuel's right hand so severely that she had to have it amputated.

While the horror inside went on, the Pinkertons waited with drawn guns for Frank or Jesse. But neither of the brothers was there. Before the local authorities arrived, the detectives had slipped off into the night, leaving a pistol with the letters P.G.G. (Pinkerton Government Guard) on the ground to let Jesse and the Youngers know that the killing of Wicher, Lull, and Daniel had been at least partly avenged.

Public opinion was shocked. Many pesons declared that the detectives were worse than the crooks, for Jesse had never fired on women or children. One pro-South newspaper called for a revival of the Quantrill raiders to combat the Pinkertons. Even persons with Northern sentiment began to favor granting amnesty to the James and Younger brothers. A motion was introduced in the Missouri legislature to this effect. The wording is descriptive of the legend developing around Jesse James and his sidekicks—these men were "too brave to be mean; too generous to be revengeful, and too gallant and honorable to betray a friend or break a promise." They had been forced by the war's aftermath to commit acts which in wartime had been patriotic. When the amnesty resolution was put up for a vote there were fifty-eight ayes and only thirty-nine nays. But two thirds was necessary for approval so the resolution failed.

Shortly thereafter Jesse sent a letter to a newspaper in which he spoke out against the Pinkertons, who persecuted him for "blood money" paid out by the railroads. He warned Robert Pinkerton that God would one day deliver him into Jesse's hands. The unusual twist of an outlaw publishing threats in a newspaper was just another aspect of Jesse's remarkable career.

But twiddling a pen was not the life for a folk hero. Jesse really could not resist the thrill of freebooting. So on the night of July 7, 1876, he was back at his trade. Out of the woods he rode with his gang and seized a railroad watchman. Then he used his red lantern to flag down an approaching Missouri Pacific train. Once the train was stopped, the gang hopped aboard. The passengers and crew were herded into one car, where two or three desperadoes stood guard over them. The rest of the gang worked on dynamiting the express-car safe. While the passengers waited, they sang hymns. This encouraged a minister to warn the sinners among them to repent before they were murdered. The oratory may have amused the guards, but it did little to ease the passengers' concern over their future well-being. Once the booty of $15,000 had been stashed in the proper saddlebags, the gang shot up the express car just for the fun of it, then galloped off, leaving the minister, but not the passengers disappointed.

It had been a thoroughly professional job—quick, well managed, and injuring no one except the gold shippers, and few cared about them. The governor offered a paltry $300 for the capture of any bandit, a sum that no one considered worth risking his comfort for, and much less his life.

Soon after the robbery Hobbs Kerry, an uncle of the Younger brothers, attracted the attention of the authorities by a sudden spending spree. Kerry was arrested and identified as one of the gang. Under questioning he implicated the Jameses and the Youngers. In response to the publicity, Jesse sent his customary letter to the press, denying the accusation and claiming that eight of his friends could prove he was nowhere near the said train during the late unpleasantness. He was unfairly blamed for every robbery west of the Mississippi, Jesse complained.

Jesse's brother Frank was also having the time of his life robbing trains. The excitement was so stimulating that he wished to have a lady to share the good times with, in particu- lar cute Annie Ralston. One day the girl packed her trunk and told her parents that she was taking the train to visit their relatives in Kansas City. Smiling Frank was on the train, not to rob it for a change. He married the girl and sometime later she sent the following one-line announcement to her astonished parents: "I am married and going West. Annie." The first time her parents learned the actual identity of their son-in-law was when twelve detectives ransacked their home, searching for the James gang.

In the summer of 1876 things became a little dull for the gang, so they decided to pay a visit to a bank at Northfield, Minnesota. Here, for the first time, events did not progress in the accustomed manner. Perhaps the several quarts of whiskey the gang consumed before operations had some effect on their efficiency. In any event three desperadoes staggered into the bank, while two stood guard outside, and three waited on the outskirts of town. At gunpoint the three in the bank lined up the bank patrons and officials. Then the acting cashier was ordered to open the safe. When he refused, a gang member put a knife to his neck. The brave man still refused, so the bandit had no choice except to slash his throat, then shoot him just for good measure. When the bullets started popping, a teller ran from the building. A gang member bade him fare- well with a bullet, which was aimed at his back but merely went through his shoulder, allowing the man to escape.

With all the shooting, the townsfolk became aware that someone was trying to make off with their money. Guns came out of closets, and soon bullets began splatting around the two bandit guards outside. The crooks fired back, and Nicholas Gustavson, a confused Swede who did not understand the shouting in English, was plugged. Now the three reinforce- ments galloped into town, their guns blazing. But the townsfolk, firing from cover, brought down two desperadoes. The rest made their escape through a bee swarm of bullets.

Telegraph wires buzzed with news of the holdup, and the greatest manhunt in Minnesota history began. Word that the gang was made up of the Jameses and Youngers did not deter the Minnesotans, for this was a northern state devoid of sympathy for Confederate renegades. After several days four gang members were captured. Among them were Cole, Bob, and Jim Younger. All were sentenced to life imprisonment.

Frank and Jesse had escaped, but the carefree days were over. With the Youngers gone, their interest in bandit deeds waned. They were hunted men, for the Pinkertons and government law enforcers were constantly on the prowl for them. Their friends and mother were almost always under surveillance. Jesse, with his wife and two small children, posed as Thomas Howard, a railroad man in search of work. Even so, only the fact that there was no picture of him (just the one his mother kept concealed in a locket beneath her blouse) prevented him from being caught. He was by now thirty years old—in early middle age. He had no real occupation—only that of master thief. And so he was forced to continue his robberies, though now they were little more than dangerous drudgery.

On October 7, 1879, Jesse and four men hit a train at Glendale, Missouri, grabbing enough loot to keep Jesse out of the trade for a couple of years. But by the summer of 1881 economic necessity forced him back into the business. Fifty-four miles northeast of Kansas City, Jesse, Frank, and three others purchased tickets and climbed on board the smoking car. It was nearly nine o'clock at night when the train stopped at Winston, Missouri. The brakeman walked down the track behind the last car to flag any train that might be approaching. Conductor Bill Westfall waited until all the new passengers were aboard, then he swung a highball lantern to signal the engineer to put the train in motion. The ponderous drive wheels began to turn, and the train jerked forward. Westfall watched the brakeman catch the rear handrail, then he turned to enter the car. As he did, a revolver was poked into his stomach, and a gruff voice ordered him to throw up his hands.

Westfall was terrified, for he had helped the railroad search for the James gang, and he knew he was a marked man. He twisted away from the gun just as it went off. Then he shoved the bandit away from him and dashed down the aisle. The bandit took aim with a pistol in his right hand, but the weapon caught on a bell cord, and the shot went wild. The outlaw had a second gun in his left hand, and this bullet hit Westfall in the back. The conductor flung up his arms, staggered out the door, and toppled out onto the embankment—dead.

While the outlaws' attention was on Westfall, a muscular stonemason employed by the railroad sprang from his seat, a heavy tool in his hands. But before he could strike, a gang member put a bullet through his head. With that all the passengers ran for safety toward the rear of the train. Once there they began frantically to hide their valuables. The brakeman in the last car yanked the cord that controlled the air brakes, forcing the train to a lurching halt.

Jesse ran to the locomotive, demanding that the engineer get the train moving, for they were close enough to the station that the shooting might be heard and a posse might be forming. The plucky engineer, ignoring the pistol Jesse waved in his face, insisted that the brakeman had deactivated the air brakes when he had pulled the cord. Work must be done on the brakes before they would release. While the engineer was talking, the fireman jumped out of the cab. Then, with Jesse's attention turned to the fireman, the engineer hurled the lantern out, leaving the cab in shadows. As Jesse groped about, the engineer ducked onto the running board and doused the big headlight on the front of the engine. Now it was totally dark, and there was no way Jesse or his men could get the train rolling again. Jesse was losing his touch.

But the crooks were not yet ready to admit defeat. They hurried to the express car, where they forced the messenger to open the safe. But to their immense disappointment there was only $600 in currency—hardly enough to pay their traveling expenses to and from the robbery site.

"Where's the rest?" a bandit snarled at the messenger.

"There's no more except those silver bricks," the man stammered. An outlaw lifted one of the bricks, but it was so heavy that he knew it would be useless to try to carry it off.

The outlaws were furious. Here was a fortune in silver, and they could not take it. And the passengers must have several thousand dollars in money and jewelry, but they didn't dare take the time to search them. With a great deal of muttering they reluctantly climbed down from the express car and vanished into the night.

It was getting so that the cash collected was nowhere commensurate with the danger to which Jesse was exposed. Still, he had his career as well as his reputation to consider. So he plotted another train robbery—his last, although he didn't know it.

Jesse's fatal mistake was not in holding up the Chicago & Alton on September 7, 1881. The gang had no trouble stopping the train and forcing the messenger to open the safe (although, once again the loot was trifling—so much so that the enraged outlaws beat the messenger senseless with their pistol butts). Jesse's mistake was to take on a young recruit named Charles Ford. Soon, Charles and his boyishly handsome brother Bob were staying in Jesse's home in St. Joe, Missouri, where they entertained themselves plotting a bank heist. But Bob was after bigger game. He wanted the juicy $20,000 reward offered by the railroads for Jesse, dead or alive.

Bob Ford had been in contact with the new governor of Missouri as well as the Kansas City police commissioner. He probably reasoned that it would be easier to shoot Jesse in the back than to continue the dangerous game of robbing trains and banks. Possibly Bob envied Jesse's fame and assumed some would wash off on him when he brought Jesse's career to an end. In any event Bob waited for the proper moment, and on the morning of April 3, 1882, it came.

Zee James prepared breakfast for her husband, the two Fords, and her two children. After the meal Jesse and Charlie Ford went to the stable to curry their horses—for Jesse always wanted his steed ready for a quick getaway. It was hot, but Jesse kept his coat on so that no passerby would notice the two revolvers strapped to his hips. When they returned to the house, Jesse removed his coat and vest. Then, feeling perfectly safe with the armed Fords, he unbuckled his pistols, "for fear somebody will see them if I walk in the yard." These were to be his last words.

Tossing his weapons onto a bed, he looked up at a picture of Skyrocket, the horse he had loved above all others. How many times had that stupendous animal carried him beyond his pursuers! Then he noticed that the picture had a coating of dust on it. He turned his back to the Fords, picked up a cloth, and stood on a chair to wipe the picture. At that moment both the Fords drew their guns. Bob pulled the trigger, and as he did so, Jesse heard the click of the firing pin. Instantly he sensed danger and tried to leap to safety. But it was too late. Ford's gun roared, and Jesse fell as a bullet pierced his skull. His wife ran into the room screaming, while the Fords scurried out.

At first no one believed that it was Jesse James who was dead.

But then they found a gold watch on the corpse which had been taken during a stagecoach robbery. Also the house was filled with mementos of Jesse's active life. And the horses and saddles in the stable belonged to persons all over the trans-Mississippi region. Once it was determined that the dead man was indeed the legendary outlaw, newspapers ran sentimental headlines like "Good-bye, Jesse!" A special train carried the body to the funeral home in Kearney. Here hundreds of friends as well as curiosity seekers viewed the corpse. At the service the minister began his eulogy with the biblical quotation: "Man that is born of a woman is of few days, and full of trouble." It was eminently suitable as Jesse's adieu.

After Jesse's passing, Frank James settled down with his wife Annie. He was acquitted after a sensational trial, although on what grounds one cannot imagine. Frank continued to live peacefully until he died many years later. As for the Fords, they received the reward but with it the hatred and contempt of everyone. Charlie at last shot himself, and Bob was later killed by a relative of the Younger brothers in a Colorado saloon.

The breakup of the James gang signaled the closing of the era of train robberies. The railroads had simply outgrown the old-time shoot-'em-up bandit. Express cars were built heavier, and safes became much more difficult to crack. Railroad detectives became quite efficient. The perfection of telegraph communication gave robbers less time to consummate their deeds. Photography progressed so that it was easy to circulate accurate pictures of the wanted men. By 1900 train robberies had dropped to twenty-nine per year. By 1905 there were only seven. A colorful, but brief, era in American railroading was over.

10

Song of the Rails

Hank Chrysler was a brawny engineer who carried a pistol on his hip while he was at the throttle. He drove a locomotive for the Union Pacific eastward out of Ellis, Kansas, every morning and back at night. Hank drove his locomotive hard like a cowboy his mustang. He kept to his schedule—come snow, come rain, come any dang Jesse James who dared contest his right-of-way—but he did not burn out his boilers the way some swashbuckling engineers did. He loved the great iron dragon and never raced her mercilessly. He never let her flues cake with lime, and he kept her well oiled so her wheels almost floated over the rails. When the UP changed from the spark-belching wood burners to the new coal locomotives, Hank was given the honor of piloting the first of the sleek beasts through his area.

Sometimes Hank would take his son on the run with him. Young Walt, not yet in his teens, would sit in the cab, watching down the line of rails that stretched out across the sighing Kansas grasslands. Walt always regarded the trip home as the most fun, for it was dark then and the world took on a mystic glamour as the engine roared forward, cleaving the darkness with its headlight, shattering the stillness with its whistle and the thunder of its steam pistons. Years later Walt wrote of these trips in an autobiographical book entitled *Life of an American Workman:*

At my father's nod the fireman would leap to sweaty action, swinging back the fire door with a devilish clang. In that moment of glare, each face in the cab turned as red as an Indian mask. With frantic grace the fireman would scoop coal from the tender, swinging the big shovel so expertly that the lumpy succession of black galaxies went in tight clusters to the center of the white-hot fire. Out side the engine cab the night would seem to moan and scream every time my father pulled the whistle cord. I watched the muscles writhe below the hair on his forearms when he used his hands to turn a cock or pull the throttle farther back upon its quadrant. I watched his face when he fixed his gleaming eyes in a gaze ahead into the headlight's yellow corridor through which we rode. The padded board on which I huddled bounced and throbbed and shook from side to side. Hot cinders bit me on the face.

On and on they went through the dark enchantment. Once in a while Walt could yank the whistle cord that sent the plaintive "hooo-eee" flowing like liquid around them. Walt loved everything about those nighttime rides. To him it was one of life's perfect experiences.

When Walt finished high school in 1892, his father wanted him to go to college. Walt resisted. He was not one who could sit for long listening to palaver about the march of dead armies or the cadence of poetic meters. Fleets of trains were his armies and the clack of their wheels were his rhythms. Railroading was in his blood, and not even his father's gruff arguments could force him into college. Instead he took a job as a janitor in the Union Pacific shop. The pay for ten hours' labor was one single dollar.

But Walt loved it. While he swept the floor and emptied the trash, he watched the mechanics take apart the locomotives that came in for repair. He gazed in fascination as the fireboxes were pulled out, as steam chests were disassembled, as boilers were drained, and flues removed for cleaning. He was assigned the job of lugging the sixteen-foot-long iron flue tubes over to the timber shed, where they were cleaned. Because the flues carried hot gases from the firebox the length of the locomotive boiler, they accumulated a thick deposit of alkali from the water that surrounded them. This alkali prevented the gases rushing through to the smokestack from transmitting their heat to the boiler water. To remove the alkali, men in the timber shed rolled the flue tubes down piles of logs until the material cracked off. When the thumping and clanging and general turmoil was over, Walt dutifully toted the iron pipes back to the shop, where they were reinserted into the boiler.

In six months Walt went to the master mechanic, who ran the shop, and asked if he could begin a four-year machinist apprenticeship. The master accepted him, and Walt went home that evening so charged up with excitement that he could hardly hold a dinner knife. "I was shivering in my eagerness," was the way he remembered it.

To be a Union Pacific apprentice was a great honor for a boy just out of high school. It gave him prestige in the community. "You can bet that I was proud!" Walt admitted. There was a stiff examination, for locomotives were precision machines, and it took a person with mechanical aptitude to be able to repair them. After he passed the exam, Walt made himself a set of tools. His most important one was a pair of calipers, which, when spread to their limit, could measure a diameter of four inches. He then made a depth gauge for measuring holes. Later he fashioned a pair of granddaddy calipers, with legs almost as long as his arm. Once he had these, he began helping on the big lathe where the locomotive piston rods were turned. An old-timer in the shop made him a beautiful toolbox.

Walt was a serious young man, and worked sixty hours a week. Most of the time he was in the roundhouse pit, where the mechanics stood beneath the tracks to remove parts from the locomotives. Walt labored with soot on his face and grease splattering his hands and clothing. But to him it was exciting to examine the innards of great beasts, silent now while they patiently waited for the mechanical doctors to make them healthy again. Lifting the parts out, then inserting them back in made Walt's muscles hard. He was a big fellow already, but now he became leather tough.

And he was cocky, he admitted that. He knew he had a special talent with things mechanical. He felt that he was part of something big, something which he described as the "unfolding magic which was then beginning to transform the continent." In his spare time he remained in the shop to work on a model locomotive more than two feet long. He made it of iron scraps to his own specifications. As the locomotive grew, he felt akin to a sculptor creating a thing of beauty out of formless pieces of material. When the thing was completed, he laid miniature rails in his backyard and sent the baby dragon chugging and snorting in a large circle. He even had a whistle in the engine, which bellowed like an unruly infant. Even Walt's father grinned as the chubby iron tyke moved boldly through the grass and dandelions.

Walt served as apprentice for one year at the modest wage of five cents an hour. The second year his pay was doubled. As he began his third year he was raised to an exciting twelve and a half an hour. He might well have continued at the shop for many years had he not flung a large glob of grease at a fellow worker during a playful fracas. The grease was in the air when a door opened, and the general foreman walked right into it—face first, of course. "He fired me before he had the stuff wiped off," Walt admitted. Although the foreman later forgave him, Walt was ready to move on to new soot pits, for here he was over twenty and had only seen the little town of Ellis, Kansas.

So he left home and headed for the Santa Fe shops in Arkansas City. Since he had good recommendations, he was hired. But the shop boss was skeptical about Walt, who seemed far too young to be as experienced as he boasted he was. The boss proposed a wage at the lowest journeyman level, which was twenty-five cents an hour. Walt insisted on the highest rate—a roaring twenty-seven and a half cents. When the boss demurred, Walt said he'd work for two weeks, then let the boss decide. But if it wasn't the highest rate, he'd quit. "A cheeky young fellow," the boss grinned to an assistant.

While the other mechanics in the Santa Fe shop watched the smart aleck with the glib tongue, the general foreman ordered him to reset the valves on a new type of locomotive, one with which Walt was unfamiliar. Walt took off the steam-chest cover and examined the valves. With his instinctive mechanical ability he could see why they were off their timing. He worked on them and soon announced to the foreman that the job was completed. The foreman walked over in disbelief. "If that engine does not pull the way she should when she's fired up—well, you won't have a job," he growled.

Walt answered back confidently, "Hook her to a string of cars; she'll take 'em away." He paused, then added wryly, "What else you got for me to do?"

The foreman didn't answer. He had the engine fired up, the cars attached, and the throttle let out. The steady *puff, puff,*

puff gave proof that Walt knew his job. The locomotive pulled the cars easily. When Walt's two weeks were up, he got top wages.

But Walt did not work with the Santa Fe for long. Soon he received a letter from the new master mechanic at the UP's Ellis shop offering him a full thirty cents an hour if he would be the night mechanic. He accepted quickly, for he missed his mother's cooking just as much as he desired the increased wages. And there was a girl named Della. . . .

As night mechanic, it was Walt's responsibility to see that each engine was put into top shape for the next day's run. This might mean that he would have his men scrub out a boiler, or caulk some flues or adjust a few air brakes or reset steam-chest valves or any number of things. When the dispatcher called for a locomotive, Walt had better have one ready.

Despite his steady advancement, Walt was restless. Ellis was too small to suit his ambitions. When he told his parents that he was considering employment in a large city, his father frowned, and his mother cried softly in her apron. Only Della seemed to understand—she with a kitten's eyes and a voice that made his insides melt like coal in a firebox. It was to Della that he confided his most cherished ambition: to be a master mechanic, head of an entire train shop! Then, after he was making a respectable salary, Della and he could get married.

Walt packed a single small suitcase with overalls and his trusty tools. His mother put up a shoebox lunch; and then he was off for Denver on a free railroad pass he had wheedled from a friend who handled UP tickets. Oh, yes, he had another piece of baggage beside his suitcase. This was nothing much— only a huge silver tuba with a golden bell.

Walt, suitcase, and dented tuba arrived in Denver twelve hours later. With his skill as a mechanic he had no trouble obtaining a job in the Colorado & Southern shop. But he didn't like Denver, particularly its whining panhandlers. Two weeks was enough. Appearing at the Union Pacific depot, he met a conductor who knew of his father. Walt asked if he'd help him get to Cheyenne. When the man answered, "I can't deadhead you, kid. Can't tell who might see me," Walt got him to take just the tuba—and leave it at the Cheyenne round-house.

Although the instrument would get a better ride than the young man who owned it, Walt was not concerned. He walked to the freight yard, where a stubby little switch engine grunted up and down the tracks pushing Cheyenne-bound freight cars into line. When the train was almost formed, Walt ran to an empty car, slid the door open, and climbed aboard. Once inside, he saw a half dozen frowsy men squatting against the car walls. One snarled at him, "Fix that door the way you found it!" Walt pushed the door so that there was an opening of seven or so inches. Then the muttering stopped, and shortly the freight began to move.

As Walt stretched out on the boxcar floor, he felt a sensation that he had never experienced before: complete freedom. No boss scowled over his shoulder. No parent voiced disapproval. He could do what he wanted—stand and watch the dusty sage pass by, or just lie back and daydream. He had a profession, could get a job when he wanted, so he had no financial woes. Besides, how much money did it take to buy a scrap of meat here and a piece of fruit there? And when he wanted to drift on there were always the boxcars where no conductors collected fares.

The vagabond life took hold of him. He worked for a while in Cheyenne, then drifted to another town. Wherever he went, he joined the local band—his trusty tuba giving each group an *oompah* it had never had before. Through the bands he met scores of young persons. He went to dances, and the ladies loved his grace. But no matter where he was, the song of the rails throbbed in his soul. Sooner or later he would con some trainman into deadheading his tuba to the next roundhouse. Then he was back on a freight, the wind ruffling his hair, adventure putting quicksilver in his veins. Laramie, Rawlins, Ogden, and points west—the towns he worked in became a blur. He used almost any excuse to quit a shop and head for the rail yard. Traveling was no longer the way to get from place to place. Instead it was a world unto itself. Riding a boxcar had an almost narcotic effect—the more he rode, the more he wished to ride.

The coins he made in the shops rolled out of his pockets like express trains running downgrade. He gave no thought to the future—only to the present and the wild music of the locomotives. He'd grab a freight for anywhere, taking only his suitcase and his tuba, not bothering to determine if he had enough cash for food. What did it matter? He'd hold his hunger until the train stopped, then walk to town. "Any time you knocked at a back door out West and explained that you were on the move, looking for work, you got something to eat; maybe just bread and butter, maybe a few slices of cold meat. No one ever felt a need to blush in those days for eating such a meal." He remembered how his own mother had constantly provided food for men drifting through the countryside.

He often used his father's name to get special treatment on the Union Pacific. By identifying himself he could sometimes ride in the caboose, where a stove kept the trainmen warm on winter days. Other times he helped with the work, a common duty being to climb atop a boxcar and turn the brake wheel to slow the train. Once in a while some kindly engineer even allowed him into the cab, where he sat on the fireman's side and rang the bell and chatted about locomotives, which was the only subject about which he had much knowledge or interest.

Walt rode the rails for several years while he poked from one Western roundhouse to the next. But it wasn't all warm breezes and smooth roadbeds. During the winter the cold was like an animal which gnawed into his bones. The boxcar floor-boards were frigid. Icy winds blew through the freight door, whether it was open or not. In the hobo jungles there was almost no protection from the snarling wind. "What a tough life it is in cold weather!" Walt admitted.

And there were the railroad brakemen and conductors who sometimes hunted down the boxcar denizens. The trainmen of certain lines came at them with heavy brake sticks. And woe to the vagabond who didn't move fast enough! Sometimes they would be forced off the train in a desolate area of snow, ice, and that dreadful Rocky Mountain wind. And then one day Walt lost his beloved tuba.

A UP foreman had sent the instrument to Walt in Pocatello, Idaho. But Walt had stayed in Pocatello only a few days before he had had enough of the chilly gale that pocked his face with ice and cinders. He had hurriedly hopped a freight south, forgetting his instrument until he reached Salt Lake City. He refused to go back to hated Pocatello for anything, even his tuba. And so it sat in the Short Line roundhouse like a lonely puppydog patiently waiting for a master who would never return. Walt felt bad. "I hope whoever became its master learned to play it sweetly," was his lament.

Walt reached Salt Lake in 1900. He was now twenty-five years old. The Denver & Rio Grande hired him at thirty cents an hour. Although he liked Salt Lake as well as his job, he was lonely for Della, had always been lonely for her. Her letters had found him in a dozen paint-peeling hotels. He carried them with him to reread during the bleak nights on the trains. And when he was especially lonely, he would hold the letter packet close to his face and breathe in Della's faint perfume. Then he seemed to feel her scented hair brush his cheek.

He gave up roaming, worked steadily, and saved his money. A year later he had enough for a new suit of clothes and a fancy derby hat. In this finery he went to the railroad station and bought a passenger ticket—the first he had purchased in his entire life. He rode back to Ellis and Della's willing arms. They had a quiet church wedding, and at midnight caught the train for Denver. He rented a house there, which he filled with $170 worth of furniture purchased on time. Yes, he had really settled down at last.

Once Walt turned from riding the rails to pursuing his mechanical interests, his career veered upward. Within less than a year he was shop foreman of the Salt Lake roundhouse with his own hole-in-the-wall office, a telephone that occasionally worked, and ninety men to order around. One year later he was offered a job with the Colorado & Southern as general foreman. Now there were more than a thousand men under him—engine crews, shop repairmen, carmen, and roundhouse workers. And his pay was up to one hundred and forty dollars a month. His reputation for running a top-rate shop grew and it was not long before he got a wire from Fort Worth asking him to take charge of an entire division as master mechanic. His dream had come true, and he was still under thirty!

The story should end here, but it doesn't. Walt loved anything mechanical, and when those newfangled automobiles began bucking down the roadways, he looked them over and decided he could make them about as well as anybody. He apprenticed himself at General Motors, then hit out on his own. The result was a new giant in the field. Of course the cocky upstart named his huge auto company after himself: Chrysler Motors.

Not everybody who rode the rails could quit vagabonding the way Walt Chrysler had. Life on the rails had far too much appeal. They worked only until the boredom of the job or the web of a female made them uncomfortable. Then they found it easy—oh, so easy—to saunter to the freight yard and hop onboard a boxcar. The swaying of the car and the lullaby of the wheels made them feel contented. As long as the freight kept moving, the rest of the world, with its terrible responsibilities, was kept at bay. Their destination was incidental; it was the motion that was the reason for existence.

The hobo life that evolved around the trains was truly an experience unto itself. Just waiting in the freight yard for an empty car was a thrill:

Lying there resting, I began to notice the sights and sounds around me. The city's constant noise . . . was excluded. . . . Silence prevailed except for footsteps on the roadbed. There was no movement and the silence was completely absorbing. Barely audible in the distance was the idling engine near the tower, a constant level droning that almost blended into the quiet.

Soon a switch engine moved past, a crescendo of sound that quickly faded into the rumbling silence that was the normal tone of the yard. A hobo would secretly watch while the freight train was assembled. The switch engine did the work, removing a boxcar from one track, then taking it to the head of the yard, which rose a few feet above the rest of the area. The engine would give the car a push and from there it would glide soundlessly on its own along the downgrade track, with yardmen throwing switches so that it ended in the correct line. When the car reached the others, it clanged into the head of the line with a tremendous crash as the couplings banged together. A chain reaction followed, with each car jolting into the next down the line. When the last car had been bumped, there was silence again.

After the train was made up, the engineer gave three whistle blasts. Before the train started, a waiting hobo would hurry to an empty boxcar, which he had already picked out, toss in his small suitcase and bedroll, and climb aboard. For the first-time rider, this moment of departure was never to be forgotten:

The train moved through the outskirts of the nearly deserted city . . . wind rushing by—this was it! All my expectations were filled in these moments. I could ride forever. [Thus did a Harvard graduate vagabond, Mike Mathers, recall taking to the road.]

A boxcar usually collected many riders at the yards and water stops. Most of these men shared a common love of travel. As the train moved out, some would sit in the car doorway with their legs dangling over the side, watching the endless procession of farms, towns, rivers, hills, and forests sweep past. Others would stand behind them, shuffling from one side of the car to the other in order to enjoy the best vista. The rest would slouch against the car walls, letting the rocking rhythm of the train lull them to sleep. They would call each other by colorful nicknames—never asking for a last name, which would break their unspoken pledge to divorce themselves from the work-a-day world. There was Shorty or Whiskers or Lefty—common handles. Or there was Bacon Bill, Wahoo, Plato, or Inner Tubes—the latter called after the auto tubes he wore on his feet in place of shoes.

Some of the men were tramps and some hoboes. The tramps did not work, they lived off handouts. The hoboes could panhandle as well as any tramp, but they also earned money from temporary jobs. Hoboes followed the seasons, cherry picking in the early summer, or bunching onions or scooping beets, drifting to wherever the wheat or corn or grapes were being harvested. But whether they were tramps or hoboes, they knew that money was created to be spent, not hoarded, and rarely did a coin jingle in a pocket for long. The fact that everybody in a boxcar was broke, or very near to it, created a camaraderie seldom found in other professions. Did a man have some redeye left in his bottle? Why, sure he'd share it. Did he have tobacco fixings from butts he had collected around a depot? Of course, his buddies of the moment could have a puff, more than one if they wanted.

At the hobo jungles in the brush beside the yards it was the same. Somebody always had a frying pan, which they called a banjo, and every pal could toss his grub into it. Just naturally a few fellers hunted up wood for a fire. And hoboes before them had fixed a stone fireplace, with a grill made of abandoned pieces of metal. There was coffee for all, if anyone had had the money and the forethought to purchase or panhandle some the day before. Breakfast would often be fried potatoes filched from a field or found loose in a boxcar. And there was oatmeal, made with hot water, sprinkled with sugar sometimes but no milk.

Hoboes thrown together by chance would often find a note of congeniality among themselves. Then one would say, "How 'bout a Frisco Circle?" With that he would draw a large oval in the dirt, and the rest would toss in whatever money they could, even if it was only a couple of pennies. It was the sharing, not the size of the contribution, that counted. Several of the men would take the money and walk into town, each concentrating on a particular grocery store, so to get as much for his meager funds as possible. He'd usually approach the back entrance and give the owner a pitiful story about his destitution and his gnawing need for food. Because the hobo said he didn't want charity but intended to pay for whatever he received, it took a glacial-hearted grocer not to donate much more than the hobo's nickels would actually purchase. When each foraging party returned, they put their food into a large kettle. There was usually a bountiful harvest, four or five times more delectables than an ordinary housewife could have gotten for the same amount. The whole conglomeration was boiled for several hours. When a savory fragrance announced that the brew was done, the hoboes dug into a most delicious Mulligan stew. It was the highlight of any jungle evening.

The jungles were surprisingly clean, at least during the era of steam when the railroads were the prime means of travel. The jungle was swept each day with a broom made of branches. There were nails on the trees for hanging clothes and cooking utensils. The hoboes washed their clothes in the stream near which the jungle was inevitably located and they hung their wash to dry on ropes that earlier residents had scavenged from someplace or other. The art of scavenging also enabled most jungles to have a permanent inventory of soup kettles, cooking pots, and tin spoons. Everyone could use them, but they had to be washed afterward. In many jungles a mirror was hung on a tree, often even with a razor beside it. The men tried to keep themselves reasonably well-shaven, although a two-or-three-day stubble was not uncommon. Because the jungles were so well equipped, a man on the move did not have to overburden himself with heavy gear.

Upon entering a jungle each hobo submitted to certain unwritten rules. He never prodded another about his past. He had to do his part to keep the jungle a place where respectable, although down-and-partially-out, men could reside in dignity. And he could never walk off with the jungle's utensils or another man's gear. In the days before the deterioration of the railroads, a man could leave his pack in the jungle, go off to town for a day, and return to find the pack not only safe but in exactly the same position in which he had deposited it.

In the morning, a hobo would disentangle himself from his waterproof bedroll, guzzle coffee brewed in the community pot, then prepare either for another day of camp life or for a swing back on the rails. When he hopped a boxcar, often he didn't know where it was headed, and more than once he might expect to be feeling southern zephyrs only to end up humping over the frigid Rockies. This could be serious, for blankets had to be winter-thick to protect one from the mountain winds slicing through the boxing boxcar. But most hoboes could take it, for living outdoors had long since acclimated their bodies to nature's rigors. They were all lean and hardy men, their faces creased by the elements. They could squat in a November rain and scarcely feel the chill.

When a hobo was choosing a railroad car, he did so with care, for they were not all the same. Mike Mathers, our Harvard vagabond, recalled one of his worse rides, this on an open gondola loaded with steel pipes. The train was picking up speed when Mathers' gondola began to rock:

It would have been too cold to sit on top of the pipes so I decided to lean against the back of the gondola, keeping my eye on the pile. A few moments later, the train lurched forward, and a pipe shot out from the top of the pile, slamming into the back just a foot from my left shoulder. In no time I scurried to the top of the pile.

But now Mike found that the ride was far worse than before. The pipes were jiggling so that his teeth chattered. Each bounce of the pipes lifted him three inches into the air, and landed him with a thump right on the steel floor. It grew even colder, yet the vibration of the gondola made it difficult to keep his blanket wrapped around his shoulders. It felt as if his insides were being turned into an icy mush. Yet the bouncing continued without letup—and it grew colder. He had no idea when the horrible ride would end. "It was a nightmare," was his final comment.

The devastating ride was only three hours, but it seemed to Mike he had been on the gondola since the Ice Age. When the train slowed to twenty miles an hour, he leaped off. And there he was, somewhere in Illinois, far from a town or a jungle. He began walking down the tracks, completely alone in the dark, uncaring country. Many hoboes had similar experiences.

Others were not even so lucky as Mike when it came to riding with a load of pipes. One hobo remembered the scared-est he had ever been. It was when he boarded a pipe gondola outside Kansas City. He seated himself on the top of the pipes, ready to move at an instant when they began to shift. Then he looked down and saw two hoboes sleeping on the deck. Knowing their danger, he yelled to them. But they didn't respond. So he crawled along the pipes, hollering all the time above the clatter of the freight. Still he couldn't rouse either of them.

When he reached the bottom, he was angry, for he didn't like a couple tons of unstable steel above him. He grabbed one of the men and shook him. Then he discovered that the man's arm was as stiff as a tree limb. With a jolt he realized that he was dead, and had been for some time. He almost choked with revulsion as he saw that the other man was dead, too. He scrambled up the pipes. There had been no blood; both hoboes must have been crushed internally when one or more of the pipes had pounded against them. The living hobo spent the rest of the trip shivering in his perch, trying not to glance at the pair of corpses. He did not sleep that night.

A hobo rider never knew when he would have an eye-popping experience. "We was going down through Southern California in the desert on the Southern Pacific," one vagabond recalled. "There was four of us in this boxcar, and we're drinkin' wine. We're all about half-drunk. All at once I looked out the door sideways like this and I see boxcars stacking up like matches. Man! I figger someone's having a hell of a wreck down there." As the hobo's boxcar came to a squealing halt, he saw cars careening off into the desert, twisting and turning, breaking up against boulders, smashing, splintering into shreds. The noise of fragmenting wood and metal was ear shattering. It was a stupendous, devastating crash. No one riding any of the cars could have survived.

Then the brakeman came back and said, "If I was you people, I'd get outa here." The hobo asked how come and the brakey answered: "We got cars strung all over the desert."

The hobo gasped as he asked the brakeman if that wreck was his train. The brakey nodded. "The car next to you was the last one off the track."

The hobo's jaw dropped, and the wine evaporated from his brain. "Boy, you talk about sober; I sobered just like that. I said, man, I quit the rails!"

In the jungles there was almost always a man named Stumps or Fingers, due to the fact that he had lost a limb or two as the result of a bad freight hop. Catching a moving train was tricky. It was usually going faster than a man thought, and when he grabbed hold he got a nasty jerk that sometimes snapped his feet off the ground. If his grasp was not secure, he would fall, and the heavy iron car wheel might sever a limb with the ease of a butcher slicing tenderloin. It was even more difficult leaving a moving car. The hobo had to hang from the doorway, letting his feet touch the ground. Then he bounded with gazelle quickness, tilting backward to counterbalance the forward rush. When he let loose, he had to pray that his legs would be able to maintain the sprint. If not, he would sprawl face forward, against the splintery wooden ties or, with a twist of an ankle, under the buzz-saw wheels.

The hobo jungles could be dangerous places when mean characters arrived. There was, for instance, the story Blackey told. He had just sold his auto for $2,200 and hit the nearest hobo hideout to celebrate. Although there were only four men present, Blackey didn't let the lack of partners hamper his mood. Wine and assorted booze were bought, with Blackey's money, of course. As the festivities progressed, it dawned on one of the men that Blackey had a rather considerable bankroll somewhere on his person. While Blackey was swapping railroading tales with the others, the scoundrel eased into the brush, where he found a heavy two-by-four. Quietly he approached Blackey from the rear. Raising the club, he swung for Blackey's head. Perhaps the wine distorted his aim, for the blow only grazed Blackey. As the thug raised his arm for another try, Blackey yanked a knife from his boot and lunged at his adversary. The blade stabbed into the attacker's heart, and he fell dead.

Ordinarily such a murder would go unnoticed, for many hoboes carried knives, and local authorities did not fritter away their time on nameless cadavers in weedy ditches. But a passing brakeman, witnessing the incident, summoned a railroad cop. Blackey was brought in and sentenced to ten years for second-degree murder.

Railroad hoboing was a hard life. But for most it had rewards far in excess of the rigors and dangers. There was no better way to remove oneself from society with its nagging demands and insistent harassments. Life on the rails was one of almost complete freedom. A man worked only when he wanted to. Travel was free, lodging was free, and even the food was usually free. If a hobo got too cold or hungry, he could drift into one of the religious missions that prayed and hymned along the main lines. But the very freedom sometimes made a fellow lonely. For this reason many hoboes adopted a dog. These flop-eared mutts were pathetic strays, as dissociated from the world as the hoboes themselves. Usually the dogs were small, for a man catching a boxcar preferred an animal he could toss aboard with as much ease as his tattered suitcase. Yet sometimes a hobo's friendship for his dog blurred his judgment. One result was the Charlie Chaplinesque scene Lefty witnessed.

Lefty was waiting for a freight in the Sante Fe yard when up came an old tramp with a pair of hounds as tall as his hip. A tough railroad cop approached. The "bull" asked the old man if he really thought he'd hop the freight with those huge dogs. When the old man said yes, the bull scrutinized the hounds and the height of the boxcar roof where the old man planned to ride. Go on up, the cop motioned, curious to see how the old timer would raise the dogs on the steep ladder.

The dogs were tied together with a short rope around their necks. The old man put the rope over his shoulders, took a firm hold on the iron ladder rungs, and began pulling himself up. The dogs kicked and squirmed as they dangled in the air, the rope almost strangling them. They barked frantically and twisted their necks. Their hind feet treaded air as if they were practicing the ballet. The old hobo slipped and staggered on the ladder. Sweat beaded his face, but he kept inching upward. At last he reached the top. The three of them—the man and his two hounds—lay there as exhausted as if they had scaled Mount Everest. The bull climbed up the ladder, and it would not have surprised Lefty if he had tossed them off; some bulls were just that mean. Instead the bull reached in his coat and pulled out a camera. He got the group in his sights and clicked the picture. As the burly cop walked off, Lefty heard him chuckle all the way down the line.

Whatever it was about riding the rails, it got in one's blood. Longtime hoboes became so addicted to the clack of the rails that they found it impossible to sleep without this sound. But there came a time when arthritis, asthma, or just plain old age made it impossible to continue the vagabond life. Mike Mathers met a seasoned hobo called Whiskers who, when his drifting days were over, simply holed up in a rocky crevass beside the railroad tracks. Although his abode was merely a ticky-tacky assortment of boards, corrugated metal, and general junk, it was home not only to Whiskers, but to an almost endless assortment of guest hoboes who sought out the chatty old-timer.

For others the break was more absolute, and far more wrenching. There was Lefty, who knew he couldn't take the hard life any longer and for five years had played the family man with his wife and children in Albany, New York. But when the children grew up, the wail of the trains tugged at him. He told his wife he just had to make one last run to the Pacific and back. So he left his comfortable bungalow and clambered aboard an outward-bound freight. He was young again, it seemed. He loved the gritty taste of smoke in his mouth. He laughed at the hardships, just as he had in his younger days. But Lefty was just an old vagrant to the police who arrested him in Laramie, Wyoming. After twenty-one days in a stinking hoosegow, he realized he was tired, and his bones pained him, and the vigor of half a century ago could never be recaptured. He left the jail a broken man. Stumbling to the yards, he had to be helped into an eastbound boxcar. He had loved life on the rails, how he had loved it! But the end of the line had come.

Afterword

Suddenly they were gone—all these dragons that had thundered across the countryside for more than a century. The diesel engines, silently, efficiently, and grimly, bested the snorting iron beasts and within a few years sent almost all of them to the scrap yards. Only a few still linger, subdued now as they chug dutifully along short lines to delight children. Never again will their whistles bellow out unfettered. Never again will the expresses rumble into stations, filling the air with their smoky breath and the heat of their steamy bodies.

Yet in the minds of many persons the steamers still clatter down the tracks. I can picture the days when we lined the road to see the fabled "400" Limited streak by at more than a mile a minute, roaring like Hercules as it scattered cinders around us. The spectators (it seemed like there always were some) stood in awe as the mighty engine shot past. And when it was gone, they clapped. Sometimes I wonder what happened to the "400," that monarch of the rails. I hope the bands were playing when it made its last run.

Index

Acworth (Yankee raid), 89
Adams, John Quincy, 26
Albany, 39, 44, 53, 83
Alleghany—
   hamlet, 55
   Indians, 55–58
   valley, 38, 57
Allen, Horatio, 48
Alvord, Burt, 184
American Railway Union, 167–171
American river (Pullman coach debut), 121
"America's Appian Way," 47
Andrews, Jim (Union spy), 85–97
Appomattox Court House, 102
Army of the Cumberland, 85
Ashley, Lew, 66
Atlanta—
   junction, 82, 84–87
   city, 98–100
Averell, Mary, 143

Baltimore, 26, 82
Baltimore & Ohio Railroad (B&O), 12–20, 22–26, 37–38, 98, 161
Battle of Bull Run Creek, 84
Beauregard, General, 83, 92–93
Benjamin, Judah, 85
Ben Wright & Company, 40
Big Muddy River, 69
Big Shanty station, 87–89, 99
Black Friday, 144
"Bloody Kansas" era, 185
Bogard, John, 184
Bracken, Pete (engineer), 91–97
Brady, Jack (outlaw), 181–184
Brewster, John, 65

Bridgeport accident, 28
Browning, Sam (outlaw), 181–184
Brush, Daniel, 24–25, 65–72
Buell, Don Carlos, 85–86, 88, 98
Buffalo, 38, 83
Burlington Line, 29, 156, 158, 163

Cairo, 61, 64, 68–69, 78–79, 84, 147
Calhoun switch-out, 91–93, 99
California Development Corporation, 154
Camden & Amboy line, 31, 53
Canadian Pacific freight car, 164
Carbondale, 66–71
Cascade Bridge, 41–42, 54
Central Pacific, 115, 151–154, 161
Charleston, 101
Chattanooga, 85–91, 97–98
Chatterbox, The, 103
Chemung valley, 57
Chesapeake & Ohio Railroad, 26
Cheyenne (Pullman debut), 111
Chicago, 59, 61, 64, 72–74, 82, 163–165, 171
Chicago & Alton line, 197
Chicago & Northwestern line, 62, 161
Chicago, Burlington & Quincy line, 156
Chicago's Illinois Central depot, 9
Chicago River, 61–63
Chicago-to-Cairo food stops, 78
Chickamauga Creek, 87, 96
Chinese railroad workers, 115, 120
Cholera danger, 64, 73
Chrysler, Hank (engineer), 200
Chrysler Motors, 209
Chrysler, Walt, 200–209
Cincinnati, 82, 85

Citation of Merit (Erie Railroad), 56
Civil War and the railroads, 83–102
Cleveland (Lincoln's campaign), 83
Cleveland, Grover, 171
Colorado & Southern line, 209
Colorado River dam break, 154
Columbia, 101
Columbus (Pullman debut), 106–107
Comic Almanac, The, 103
Conestoga wagon coach, 18–19
Confederate Army, 82–83, 102
Conner, Asgill, 65, 67
Cooper, Peter, 12–20, 32–33, 60, 161
Corinth rail hub, 84
Corning town, 55
Cotton belt freight car, 164
Cuba Summit, 53, 55

Dale Creek chasm, 112–113
Dalton depot, 95, 99
Dalton Gang, 183
Davis, Jefferson, 83, 99, 102
Dayton, 56
Debs, Eugune "Dictator Debs," 167–169, 170–171
Dedham express disaster, 29
Deere, John, 73
Delaware River, 50–52, 54, 57
Denver & Rio Grande freight train, 164, (line), 208
Deposit village (beg. Erie railroad), 43, 45, 50–51
DeSoto hamlet, 65, 68–69
Dexter (May Flower accident), 34
Dickens, Charles, 7, 21
Dispatch, 188
Dodge, Colonel (Ch. engineer), 113
Douglas, Stephen, 60–61, 63, 80, 83
Dunkirk port, 40, 44, 49, 52–53, 55–56, 58
Dunleith, 79–80

East Dubuque, 79
Echo Canyon, 116
Edison, Tom, 79
Edsall, Mayor, 47
Edwards, John, 187, 189
Ellicott's Mill (first loco run), 16–19
Elmira halt, 55
Erie Canal, 12, 37, 39, 59, 74, 87
Erie Railroad—
    survey, 40–42
    bankruptcy, 47
    Citation of Merit, 56
    construction, 43
    financing, 42–44, 47–49, 51, 75
    first ride (446 miles), 45–58

Harriman's directorship, 161–162
Etowah (Civil War chase), 90
Evans and Sontag robberies, 184
Evanston (Pullman debut), 115
Ezra Church battle, 99

Farmers vs. Michigan Central, 35–36
Fillmore, Millard, 53, 55–57
First American-made locomotive, 14–20
Fish, Stuyvesant, 146
Fisk, Jim (robber baron), 144
Ford Brothers (Charles & Bob), 197–199
Fort Donelson, 84
Fort Sheridan troops, 171
Fort Sumpter, 83
"400" Limited, 220
4-4's (trains), 34
Fourth of July disaster, 30
4-4-2's (trains), 34
Fremont, 105–106
Frisbie, Charlie, 32–36, 53
"Frisco Circle," 212
Fuller, Bill (conductor), 87–97

Gads Hill robbery, 188–191
Galena & Chicago Union RR (now Chicago & Northwestern), 62
Garfield, President, 146
General (locomotive), 90–97
General Managers Association, 169
Georgia, 100–101
Georgia Central Railroad, 100, 161
Goshen, 45–48, 51, 54
Gould, Jay (robber baron), 144
Grand Island (Pullman debut), 108
Great Northern railroad, 157, 163
Great Plains (Pullman debut), 106–108
Great Salt Lake trestle, 153
Great White Father, 55
Greeley Horace, 77
Green River Bridge (Pullman debut), 114
Growing Up with Southern Illinois, 65

Harriman, Edward Henry, 143–162, 173
Harriman's Japanese negotiations, 159–161
Harriman System, 152, 154, 160
Heyming, Brace, 104–122
Hill, James, 156–157, 163, 167
Hood, John, 99–100
Hornellsville, 55
Housatonic Railroad, 59–60
House of Morgan, 156, 158
Howland, S.A., 28

Hudson River, 38–39, 44–46, 49, 52, 54, 56, 83, 161
Howells (Pullman car attendant), 104–122
Huntington, Collis, 152–153, 173

IC (Illinois Central) agents, 63, 73–75
Illinois & Michigan Canal, 64
Illinois Central Railroad—
charter, 60–61
depot, 9
Civil War part, 84–85, 98
Harriman's involvement, 146–147, 149, 161–162
overseas branch, 75
President Lincoln, 82
steamboats, 79
Illinois state, 60–64, (population surge) 73, (wealth) 75, 82
Imperial Valley flood, 154–155
Immigrant railroad workers, 63, 65, 79
Indiana, 85
Interstate Commerce Commission, 155
Iroquois indians, 55–58
Irving, Washington, 46

Jacob Schiff banking group, 148
James, Frank (outlaw), 185–188, 193–194, 199
James Gang, 187–189, 191–197
James, Jesse (outlaw), 185–188, 193–194, 199
Jamestown railroad convention, 37
"John Brown's Body," 101
Johnston, Joseph E., 83, 98–99, 100–102
Jolly Joker, The, 103
Jonesboro, 66, 69
Jones Tavern, 37–38

Kansas City Times, 187
Kearney (home of James Brothers), 186, 190–191, 199
Kennesaw Mountain, 99
Kentucky, 81
Kerry, Hobbs, 193
King, Ernie, 183–184
King, Jim, 44
Kingston, 90, 99
Knight, Bill (engineer), 88–97

Lake Erie, 38–41, 44, 52, 56
LaSalle, 61, 64
Lee, Robert E., 85, 101–102
Lefty (hobo), 218–219
Leslie, Frank, 103–122
Leslie's Illustrated Newspaper, 104
Leslie, Miriam, 103–114, 118, 122
Life of an American Workman, 200

Lincoln, Abraham, 81–85, 100
Loder, Big Ben, 49, 51–57
Lord, Eleazer, 38–39, 43–44, 48–49
Louisville supply line, 85
Luckett, Sayward, 23

Makanda hamlet, 65, 68–69
Manassas junction, 83
Manhattan Fire Insurance Company, 38
March on Atlanta, 98
March to the Sea, 100
Marietta, 85–87
Marshall city (May Flower accident), 35
Mathers, Mike, 211, 214–215
May Flower, 34–36
McDowell, General Irvin, 83–84
Memphis, 79, 84
Memphis and Charleston line (M & C), 84–85
Michigan Central railroad, 33–35, 85
Middletown, 40, 48, 54
Mimms, Zee (Jesse James' wife), 191, 198
Mississippi River, 79–80, 82, 84
Mitchel, General Ormsby, 86–90, 97
Monon of Indiana freight train, 164
Morgan, J.P., 148, 162
Mormon Church, 116
Murphysboro, 64, 66–67, 69
Murphy, Tony (engineer), 87–97

Nashville, 85–86, 98
New Jersey Central Railroad, 32–33
New Orleans, 79, 84, 151
News butchers, 78–79
New York City, 38, 42, 44–45, 47, 53–54, 82–83, 104, 157–158
New York & Erie Railroad, 39–49 (see also Erie Railroad)
New York & New Haven line, 60
New York City Council members, 46
New York Stock Exchange, 145, 158
New York rail system, 38–39, 60, 145, 163
Norris, Frank, 172
Northern Pacific railroad, 157–158, 163

Octopus, The, 173–180
Ohio lines, 95
Ohio River, 69, 74, 82, 84, 147–148
Ogden (Pullman debut), 117
Old Ironsides first salute, 13
Olney, Richard, 171
Oregon Trail, 110
Overland Express hold-up, 181–182
Owego village, 38, 55

Pacific Mail Steamship Company, 159

Panic of 1837, The, 24, 44
Pawnee Indians, 107
Peach Tree Creek battle, 99
Pennsylvania Railroad, 22, 26, 145
Petersburg junction, 101–102
Philadelphia, 22, 26, 82
Piermont-to-Goshen rail section, 47
Piermont village, 44–46, 50, 54
Pinkerton National Detective Agency, 189–192
Pittenger, Billy, 86–88, 93–96, 98
Plum Creek, 109–110
Port Jervis, 48–51, 54
Potomac River, 82
Promontory Point, 115, 118
Pullman, George, 165–171
Pullman Military Band, 166
Pullman Palace Car, 103–121, 150, 165, 167–169, 171
Pullman strike, 167–172

Quantrill Raiders, 185, 192
Quantrill, William, 185–186
Quincy line, 32, 156

Railroad accidents—
  Aaron Pratt, 29
  bridge collapse of 1840, 30
  Bridgeport, Conn., 28
  Burlington, N.J., 29
  Camden & Amboy line, 31
  Charlie Frisbie, 34–35
  Dedham express, 29
  Engineer Spencer, 30
  farmers' barrage, 36
  Hale Young, 29
  James Curtis, 29
  lumber train, 30
  Michigan ox, 35
  Springfield, 29
Railroad Avenue celebration, 56
"Railroad fashion," 28
Ralston, Annie, 194, 199
Ramapo Valley, 45, 51, 162
Randolph, Epes, 154
Resaca bridge, 87, 93–94, 99
Revolutionary War veterans, 54
Richmond, 26, 83–84, 98, 101–102
Richter, Conrad, 23
River Platte, 104
Rochester (Lincoln's campaign), 83
Rock Island Line, 62
Rocky Mountains (Pullman debut), 112
Roosevelt, Theodore, 155
Rosecrans, General William, 98
Russo-Japanese War, 159

Samuel, Reuben, 185, 190–192
Santa Fe railroad, 157, 161, 163
Savannah, 100
Schiff, Jacob, 148–149, 158, 161
Seabord Coast Line of Florida freight train, 164
Seven Wonders of the World, 51
Shanghai link with U.S., 151
Shawangunk mountains, 40, 48, 50, 55
Shawnee Hills, 69
Shenendoah Valley, 83–84
Sherman hamlet, 113
Sherman, William Tecumseh, 98–101
Skull Rocks (Pullman debut), 114
Soo Line freight car, 164
Southern Pacific railroad, 151–154, 157, 161, 172–173, 181–184, 215
South Manchurian railroad, 159
Springfield train disaster, 29
Starrucca chasm, 40; valley, 50; viaduct, 51–54
"Steam pots," 12, 24, 30, 32, 44
St. Louis, 82
St. Louis *Dispatch*, 188
Stockton & Stokes Stage line, 19

Taylor, Zachary, 56
Texas, The (locomotive), 91–93
The Town, 23
Thoreau, Henry, 26–28
Thousand Mile Tree, 117
Tom Thumb, 14–20, 32
Trans-Siberain railroad, 159
Truckee Canyon, 119–120

Union Army, 83–102
Union Pacific (UP) railroad, 104, 106, 110, 113, 117–118, 148, 162, 200, 207
U.S.S. *Michigan*, 56
U.S. Strike Commission, 169

Wabash line, 98
Walker, General L.P., 85
Washington, D.C., 53, 83–84, 155
Webster, Daniel, 53–57
Wells Fargo, 181–182
Western & Atlantic railroad, 84–86, 97–100
Whiskers (hobo), 38
Wilson, Alf (fireman), 92, 96
Wilson, John, 73–75
"Wings of Lightning," 57–58
Woodson, Governor Silas, 189–190
"Work of the Age, The," 56

Vermilion county, 74
Vicksburg, 79, 84